Qualitative Research Methods in English Medium Instruction for Emerging Researchers

This timely book will guide researchers on how to apply qualitative research methods to explore English-medium instruction (EMI) issues, such as classroom interactions, teachers' and students' perceptions on language and pedagogical challenges, and stakeholders' views on the implementation of EMI.

Each chapter focuses on a specific type of qualitative research methodology, beginning with an overview of the research and the method used, before presenting a unique case study. Chapters will also identify the process that EMI researchers went through to conduct their research, the key dilemmas they faced, and focus particularly on the methodological issues they encountered. By exploring these issues and providing up-to-date insights in contexts across the globe, this book informs theory or the lack thereof, underlying research into the phenomenon of EMI.

This text will be indispensable for researchers who want to learn and acquire skills in conducting qualitative research in EMI, as well as undergraduate and postgraduate students reading in the fields of applied linguistics and language education.

Samantha M. Curle is Assistant Professor in the Department of Education at the University of Bath, UK.

Jack K. H. Pun is Assistant Professor in the Department of English Language and Literature at the City University of Hong Kong.

Qualitative and Visual Methodologies in Educational Research
Series Editors: Rita Chawla-Duggan and Simon Hayhoe
University of Bath, UK

We are increasingly living in an era where students and researchers are under severe time pressures, whilst the amount of research topics, methodologies, data collection methods and ethical questions continue to grow. The *Qualitative and Visual Methodologies in Educational Research* series provides concise, accessible texts that take account of the methodological issues that emerge out of researching educational issues. They are ideal reading for all those designing and implementing unfamiliar qualitative research methods, from undergraduates to the most experienced researchers.

Books in the series:

- Are compact, comprehensive works, to appeal to final year undergraduates and early career postgraduates, at masters and doctoral level—both PhD and EdD. These works can also be easily read and digested by emerging, early career researchers, or raise issues applicable to experienced researchers who are keeping up with their field.
- Reflect on a single methodological problem per volume. In particular, the titles examine data analysis, research design, access, sampling, ethics, the role of theory, and how fieldwork is experienced in real-time.
- Have chapters that discuss the context of education, teaching and learning, and so can include a psychological as well as social and cultural understanding of teaching and learning in non-traditional or non-formal, as well as formal settings.
- Include discussions that engage critically with ontological and epistemological debates underpinning the choice of qualitative or visual methodologies in educational research.

The *Qualitative and Visual Methodologies in Educational Research* series includes books which stimulate ideas and help the reader design important and insightful research that improves the lives of others though education, to ultimately inspire the development of qualitative and visual methodologies.

Titles in the series include:

Multimodal Conversation Analysis and Interpretative Phenomenological Analysis
A Methodological Framework for Researching Translanguaging in Multilingual Classrooms
Kevin W. H. Tai

Qualitative Research Methods in English Medium Instruction for Emerging Researchers
Theory and Case Studies of Contemporary Research
Edited by Samantha M. Curle and Jack K. H. Pun

For more information about this series, please visit: www.routledge.com/Qualitative-and-Visual-Methodologies-in-Educational-Research/book-series/QVMER

Qualitative Research Methods in English Medium Instruction for Emerging Researchers

Theory and Case Studies
of Contemporary Research

Edited by Samantha M. Curle
and Jack K. H. Pun

LONDON AND NEW YORK

First published 2023
by Routledge
4 Park Square, Milton Park, Abingdon, Oxon OX14 4RN

and by Routledge
605 Third Avenue, New York, NY 10158

Routledge is an imprint of the Taylor & Francis Group, an informa business

© 2023 selection and editorial matter, Samantha M. Curle and Jack K. H. Pun; individual chapters, the contributors

The right of Samantha M. Curle and Jack K. H. Pun to be identified as the authors of the editorial material, and of the authors for their individual chapters, has been asserted in accordance with sections 77 and 78 of the Copyright, Designs and Patents Act 1988.

All rights reserved. No part of this book may be reprinted or reproduced or utilised in any form or by any electronic, mechanical, or other means, now known or hereafter invented, including photocopying and recording, or in any information storage or retrieval system, without permission in writing from the publishers.

Trademark notice: Product or corporate names may be trademarks or registered trademarks, and are used only for identification and explanation without intent to infringe.

British Library Cataloguing-in-Publication Data
A catalogue record for this book is available from the British Library

Library of Congress Cataloging-in-Publication Data
Names: Curle, Samantha M. (Samantha Margaret), 1983- editor. | Pun, Jack Kwok-Hung, 1987- editor.
Title: Qualitative research methods in English medium instruction for emerging researchers : theory and case studies of contemporary research / edited by Samantha M. Curle and Jack K.H. Pun.
Description: First edition. | New York : Routledge, 2024. | Series: Qualitative and visual methodologies in educational research | Includes bibliographical references and index.
Identifiers: LCCN 2023006138 (print) | LCCN 2023006139 (ebook) | ISBN 9781032451312 (hbk) | ISBN 9781032451329 (pbk) | ISBN 9781003375531 (ebk)
Subjects: LCSH: English-medium instruction.
Classification: LCC LB2331.25 .Q83 2024 (print) | LCC LB2331.25 (ebook) | DDC 428.0071—dc23/eng/20230329
LC record available at https://lccn.loc.gov/2023006138
LC ebook record available at https://lccn.loc.gov/2023006139

ISBN: 978-1-032-45131-2 (hbk)
ISBN: 978-1-032-45132-9 (pbk)
ISBN: 978-1-003-37553-1 (ebk)

DOI: 10.4324/9781003375531

Typeset in Times New Roman
by Apex CoVantage, LLC

Contents

About the editors		vii
List of contributors		viii
	Introduction: qualitative research methods in English-medium instruction for emerging researchers SAMANTHA M. CURLE AND JACK K. H. PUN	1
1	**Using Q methodology to better understand subjectivity in EMI** JIAHAO PAN AND JUN LEI	6
2	**How to conduct a multimodal classroom discourse analysis** FEI VICTOR LIM	18
3	**The use of epistemic network analysis in analysing classroom discourse in EMI-science classrooms** KASON KA CHING CHEUNG AND JACK K. H. PUN	33
4	**Using corpus linguistics and grounded theory to explore EMI stakeholders' discourse** NIALL CURRY AND PASCUAL PÉREZ-PAREDES	45
5	**Affordances of conversation analysis for investigating EMI classroom talk** REKA R. JABLONKAI	62

6 Moving beyond language in EMI research: a multimodal and multichannel analytical framework to visualise classroom practices 76
BALBINA MONCADA-COMAS AND IRATI DIERT-BOTÉ

7 A narrative enquiry into EMI instructors' linguistic and pedagogical needs 94
SEZEN ARSLAN

8 Engaged methodological approach in the study of language ideologies in EMI policies 115
PREM PHYAK, NANI BABU GHIMIRE AND MOHAN SINGH SAUD

Index 128

About the editors

Samantha M. Curle, Department of Education, University of Bath, UK Samantha M. Curle is Reader in the Department of Education at the University of Bath, UK. She completed her DPhil at the University of Oxford. She teaches subjects related to applied linguistics and is currently the director of the MRes Programme in Advanced Quantitative Research Methods. Her main research interest lies in factors affecting academic achievement in EMI. Her research has been published in journals such as *Language Teaching, Applied Linguistics Review, System,* and *International Journal of Bilingual Education and Bilingualism.*

Jack K. H. Pun, Department of English, City University of Hong Kong, Hong Kong SAR, China Dr Jack K. H. Pun is Assistant professor in the Department of English at the City University of Hong Kong. He completed his DPhil at the University of Oxford, who explored the teaching and learning process in EMI science classrooms, with a special focus on classroom interactions, use of code-switching and teachers' and students' views of EMI. His research interests lie in EMI and health communication. His research has been published in journals such as *ELT Journal, Language Teaching, RELC Journal, Journal of English for Academic Purposes* and *International Journal of Bilingual Education and Bilingualism.* He is Associate Editor of *Journal of Research in Science & Technological Education* and published two books in EMI: *Teaching and Learning in English Medium Instruction: An Introduction* (with Jack C. Richards) and *Research Methods in English Medium Instruction (with Samantha M. Curle)* by Routledge.

Contributors

***Sezen Arslan**, Bandirma Onyedi Eylül University, Turkey*
Sezen Arslan is Associate Professor in the School of Foreign Languages at Bandırma Onyedi Eylül University, Turkey. Her research interests include foreign language teacher education, specifically focusing on cultural awareness in language classrooms, assessment and evaluation and sustainable development.

***Kason Ka Ching Cheung**, Department of Education, University of Oxford, UK*
Kason Ka Ching Cheung is a Titular Clarendon Scholar, a Hong Kong Jockey Club Oxford Graduate Scholar and a DPhil student at Department of Education, University of Oxford. He is a qualified chemistry teacher in the United Kingdom and Hong Kong. He was awarded a distinction in both his PGCE/QTS at Durham University and MPhil in Educational Research at the University of Cambridge. He is an academic working in the field of nature of science, multimodal representations, visualisation and reading and writing in science. His research has been published in *Science and Education*, Research in Science and Technological Education and *International Journal of Science Education*.

***Niall Curry**, Coventry University, UK*
Niall Curry is Assistant Professor at Coventry University. His research is interdisciplinary and centres on the application of corpus linguistic approaches to different areas of applied linguistics. Among these areas is a focus on corpus-based studies of academic and scientific communication and metadiscourse in English, French, and Spanish, corpus-based contrastive linguistics, corpus-based studies of English language and language change, and corpus linguistics for Teaching English as a Second Official Language (TESOL) and language teaching materials development. He is Managing Editor of the *Journal of Academic Writing*, Section Editor of the *Elsevier Encyclopedia of Language and Linguistics*, and a Géras International Correspondent. For further details on his background, areas of interest, projects and current research, see his website niallcury.com.

Irati Diert-Boté, University of Lleida, Spain
Irati Diert-Boté is a teacher and researcher at the University of Lleida (UdL) and conducts research in different English language learning/teaching contexts, such as English for Specific Purposes (ESP) and English-medium instruction (EMI). Her research interests revolve around exploring (in)effective teaching practices in these various settings from a qualitative perspective by focusing on the affective dimension of English language learning and teaching. Her research areas include language learners' and teachers' emotions and beliefs, self-concept, identity, multimodality and plurilingualism.

Nani Babu Ghimire, Siddhajyoti Education Campus, Tribhuvan University, Nepal
Nani Babu Ghimire is a doctoral student at Tribhuvan University, Nepal. He works as Assistant Professor at Siddhajyoti Education Campus, Sindhuli. His research focuses on language ideology, agency and identity in EMI policies.

Reka R. Jablonkai, University of Bath, UK
Reka R. Jablonkai is an award-winning Senior Lecturer in Education and Applied Linguistics at the University of Bath. Her research interests include corpus-based discourse analysis, corpora in language teaching, multilingual educational contexts and intercultural communication. Her research projects were funded by BAICE and the British Council. She has published in edited volumes and journals (e.g. *ESP Today, Applied Linguistics Review*) and regularly presents at international conferences (e.g. EuroCALL, TALC, Corpora and Discourse International Conference). She is Lead Editor of *The Routledge Handbook of Corpora and English Language Teaching and Learning (2022)*. She is Liaison Officer of EuroCALL CorpusCALL SIG after acting as Chair between 2019 and 2022. She worked as a teacher trainer and a visiting scholar in various contexts in, for example, Italy, Lithuania, Germany, Slovenia, and Turkey.

Jun Lei, Faculty of Foreign Languages, Ningbo University, China
Jun Lei, PhD, is a professor in the Faculty of Foreign Languages at Ningbo University in China. His research interests include academic literacies, EMI and technology in language education. His publications have appeared in *ELT Journal, English for Specific Purposes, Journal of English for Academic Purposes, Language Learning, Language Learning & Technology, Language Policy, System,* and *TESOL Quarterly*.

Fei Victor Lim, National Institute of Education, Nanyang Technological University, Singapore
Fei Victor Lim is Associate Professor at the National Institute of Education, Nanyang Technological University, Singapore. He teaches and researches on multiliteracies, multimodal discourse analyses and digital

learning. He is an editor of Multimodality and Society and author of *Designing Learning with Embodied Teaching: Perspectives from Multimodality*, and a lead author of *Designing Learning for Multimodal Literacy: Teaching Viewing and Representing*, both published in the Routledge Studies in Multimodality.

Balbina Moncada-Comas, *Polytechnic University of Catalonia, Spain*
Balbina Moncada-Comas is Assistant Professor of English for Specific Purposes (ESP) at Universitat Politècnica de Catalunya (UPC) at the Department of Theory & History of Architecture and Technical Communication and has been a member of the research group Cercle de Lingüística Aplicada (CLA) since 2017. She teaches undergraduate technical English communication courses in the fields of engineering and optics/optometry. Her research interests are related to English-medium instruction (EMI) and ESP, language teaching/learning, identity, plurilingualism, multimodal discourse, and digital literacies (ICT). Her more recent publications have appeared in *ESP Today*, *CLIL Journal* and *IGI Global*.

Jiahao Pan, *Faculty of Foreign Languages, Ningbo University, China*
Jiahao Pan is a graduate student in the Faculty of Foreign Languages at Ningbo University in China. His research interests include English medium instruction and *Q methodology*.

Pascual Pérez-Paredes, *Universidad de Murcia, Spain*
Pascual Pérez-Paredes is Professor of Applied Linguistics and Linguistics, U. Murcia. Before this, he was Lecturer in Research in Second Language Education at the University of Cambridge. His main research interests include learner language variation, the use of corpora in language education and corpus-assisted discourse analysis. He has published extensively in journals such as *CALL, Discourse & Society, English for Specific Purposes, Journal of Pragmatics, Language, Learning & Technology, System, ReCALL* and the *International Journal of Corpus Linguistics*. He was Overall Coordinator of the MEd Research Methods Strand at the University of Cambridge (2016–2019). He is Assistant Editor of Cambridge University Press ReCALL (Q1 31 out of 187 in Linguistics).

Prem Phyak, *Chinese University of Hong Kong, Hong Kong SAR, China*
Dr Prem Phyak teaches at the Chinese University of Hong Kong. His research interests include language policy, decoloniality, translanguaging and Indigenous language education.

Mohan Singh Saud, *Kailali Multiple Campus, Dhangadhi, Far Western University, Nepal*
Mohan Singh Saud is Associate Professor of English Language Education, English language coursebook developer, ELT trainer and researcher from Nepal. He works at Kailali Multiple Campus, Dhangadhi, Far Western

University, Nepal. He is the visiting faculty at Chandigarh University, Punjab, India. He is Editor-in-Chief of *KMC Journal*. His areas of research interests include English language teaching and learning, ELT material development, teachers' professional development, EMI, teaching English as a second or foreign language, assessment, English language teachers' training and education, and linguistic diversity.

Introduction
Qualitative research methods in English-medium instruction for emerging researchers

Samantha M. Curle and Jack K. H. Pun

0.1 Introduction

The rapid trend towards globalisation has led to the expansion of English as Medium of Instruction (EMI) in secondary and tertiary education. According to a large systematic review of EMI studies (Macaro et al., 2018), approximately 74.5% of research studies have taken a qualitative research approach to exploring EMI issues. Such an expansive scope of studies shows that many EMI researchers prefer using qualitative research to examine topics, such as teachers' or students' perceptions on their EMI experiences, learners' language challenges, the factors that affect the success of EMI implementation, and stakeholder's (such as university administrators and curriculum coordinators) views on EMI policy. Other qualitative studies have explored the nature of EMI classroom interactions, teacher's talks, code-switching behaviours, and students' motivations for learning through English.

Given the popularity of taking a qualitative research approach to EMI research, this special edited volume invited emerging EMI researchers, from different parts of the world, to outline their qualitative research methods in their latest research in EMI. This volume guides readers on how to apply qualitative research methods to explore EMI issues, such as classroom interactions, teachers' and students' perceptions on language and pedagogical challenges, and stakeholders' views on the implementation of EMI. These specific topics were chosen to reflect different qualitative research methodologies that are under-represented in the current EMI literature. The aim is not only to highlight diverse qualitative research methods that might be used to research EMI but also to feature varied under-researched topics that EMI researchers can further explore.

Each chapter focuses on a specific type of qualitative research methodology, and where possible, the authors provide research instruments for future researchers to use. Every chapter begins with an overview of the research method under discussion, followed by either an in-depth explanation or critique

DOI: 10.4324/9781003375531-1

of that method, or presents a case study using that method. This volume is different from the majority of EMI books on the market as the first half of the volume (Chapter 1 to Chapter 5) provides clear explanations of how five different qualitative research methodologies may be used to research EMI. The second half of the volume (Chapter 6 to Chapter 8) provides case study examples of further three qualitative research methods as applied in an empirical piece of research. These chapters explain how the chosen research methodology and instruments were used to generate the study findings. These chapters address current central themes within EMI research and elaborate qualitative research methodologies used to investigate those themes. These chapters identify the process that EMI researchers went through to conduct their research, the key dilemmas they faced, and focus particularly on the methodological issues they encountered.

By exploring theory as well as research in practice, this volume hopes to inform theory (or the lack thereof) underlying research into the phenomenon of EMI. This volume is indispensable for EMI tutors, EMI education curriculum officers, EMI researchers, education policymakers, higher education educators, as well as undergraduate and postgraduate students reading in the fields of applied linguistics, language education and ESP, English Language Teachers (ELT) and Teaching English as a Second Official Language (TESOL).

0.2 Chapter structure and summaries

0.2.1 Chapter structure

Each chapter is structured in accordance with the approach proposed by McKinley and Rose (2016). Each chapter (where appropriate) contains the sections: (1) an overview of the project and context; (2) research plan; (3) research design; (4) method in detail (data collection, data analysis; reporting research); (5) practical lesson learned; and (6) concluding summary. As all chapters have a similar structure, the coherence of the volume is ensured. Table 0.1 outlines each of these structural aspects.

0.2.2 Chapter summaries

Chapters in this edited volume are structured according to content: literature/theoretically based chapters are presented first, followed by chapters based on empirical research (case studies). The first chapter provides a manual for doing Q research in courses taught in EMI. Q methodology adopts a person-centred approach rather than a variable-centred approach to present participants' subjective and socially shared viewpoints on complicated and/or contentious issues in a holistic design. Chapter 1 explains Q methodology, elaborates its

Table 0.1 Chapter structure

1. Project overview and context	Includes information about the substantive focus of your research project. Why were you interested in studying this topic, particularly using the methods you chose? Are the methods you chose typical for researching your topic? If not, explain your choice of methods. This section should not read as a literature review but should be a reflective exploration of your research interests.
2. Research planning	What decisions have been made when setting up the research project?
3. Research design	Includes an investigation into how you designed your study, taking into account any fundamental decisions you had to make. You should ensure that you define and explain any key terms for student readers.
4. Method in details (data collection, data analysis, and data reporting)	This should be a 'warts and all' description and evaluation of how your chosen research method actually worked in practice. What went well? What didn't go to plan? What challenges did you face? How did you respond? What would you do differently?
Practical lessons learned	This is perhaps the most important section of your research methods case study. It should be an in-depth reflection on the specific method(s) used in the research project being discussed, detailing the important lessons you learned while using this method. Student readers should be able to use these generalisable lessons to inform their own research projects.
Concluding summary	Includes a round-up of the issues discussed in your case study. This should not be a discussion of conclusions drawn solely from the research findings but should focus reflectively on the research methodology. Include just enough detail of your findings to enable the reader to understand how the method you used could be utilised by others in the same research area. Would you recommend using the particular method or, on reflection, would another method be more appropriate? What can readers learn from your experience and apply to their own research?

Source: Adapted from McKinley and Rose (2016)

philosophical and methodological assumptions, provides an applied example and rounds off by describing how it might be used in various areas of EMI research. Chapter 2 elaborates how multimodal classroom discourse analysis can be applied in the EMI classroom. This is done using the Systemic Functional Multimodal Discourse Analysis (SFMDA). Data preparation, analysis and interpretation when using this method are unpacked and discussed. Chapter 3 examines the use of an epistemic network analysis technique for content analysis to investigate how classroom interaction supports Content and Language Integrated Learning. To examine how two Hong Kong science instructors used and expanded communicative resources to promote Content and Language Integrated Learning, the authors refer to the coding scheme of a 'rainbow diagram'. Epistemic network analysis is then used to characterise the frequency of connections between the codes generated. The advantages and disadvantages of this innovative method are discussed. Chapter 4 shows how a corpus linguistics methodology can be used to analyse EMI interview data. Authors contend that using keyword analysis to produce initial open field codes for thematic analysis might help identify particular instances in focus groups and interviews where significant themes are discursively generated. The value of this approach as a means of making sense of complex EMI data is demonstrated drawing on the EMI ROAD-MAPPING theoretical framework. Chapter 5 focuses on the interactional dynamics of EMI classroom talk. The author makes the case that a conversation analysis (CA) approach is crucial to gaining knowledge and comprehension of how interactions support or obstruct the teaching and learning processes in EMI contexts. Chapter 6 discusses the application of multimodal and multichannel analysis to qualitative research in order to explore EMI classroom experiences from a micro-level perspective in Spain. This case study examines how the complexity of the teaching-learning process can be displayed through the use of a visual and qualitative methodology to study EMI practices, highlighting the need for lecturers to develop multimodal competence and multichannel awareness in order to ensure a successful meaning-making experience. Chapter 7 focuses attention on the use of narrative frames to fully comprehend the language, instructional implementation and professional development requirements of EMI educators. This case study investigates Turkish EMI teachers' linguistics and pedagogical needs, while demonstrating the usefulness of narrative frames to create reflective EMI practitioners. Chapter 8, the final chapter, discusses the methodological ways to investigate linguistic ideologies in EMI policies, building on the concept of 'engaged ethnography'. The authors use three distinct instances that depict various multilingual situations observed in Nepal. Their purpose in the chapter is to show how different engaged approaches can be utilised to study linguistic ideologies in EMI policies by engaging diverse stakeholders affected by EMI policies.

0.3 Description of the volume target reader

This edited volume provides up-to-date insights into appropriate Qualitative research methods to research EMI in contexts across the globe. This book is highly relevant to scholars in the field of educational linguistics, particularly in English language teaching, content-based instruction, Content and Language Integrated Learning and EMI. It is also valuable for the key stakeholders affected by EMI: the teachers and students. EMI practitioners can refer to this book to get ideas of how they might conduct action research on their teaching in order to enhance teaching and learning. Furthermore, any examples of research instruments with annotated notes and explanations which showcase ways of employing different Qualitative methods and techniques in researching EMI will be particularly valuable to EMI researchers and instructors doing EMI professional development courses. Undergraduate or postgraduate students doing research in this field will also find practical use in this volume. Finally, education policymakers can gain insights into how to conduct research on the effectiveness of an EMI policy being implemented in their local context. Having methodological guidelines is useful in commissioning research into policy implementation. This volume therefore caters to a diverse reader population.

1 Using Q methodology to better understand subjectivity in EMI

Jiahao Pan and Jun Lei

1.1 Introduction

English medium instruction (EMI) is defined as 'the use of the English language to teach academic subjects (other than English itself) in countries or jurisdictions where the first language of the majority of the population is not English' (Macaro et al., 2018, p. 37). Two widely envisioned goals for EMI are that students can improve their English proficiency alongside successful content learning. The past two decades have witnessed a rapid expansion of EMI across the globe, as evidenced by the exponential growth of EMI courses in all phases of education, particularly in higher education. Take China as an example. EMI can be conducted in either monolingual programmes (English alone) or bilingual programmes (both English and Chinese). In 2001, the Ministry of Education of the People's Republic of China issued guidelines to promote the quality of higher education and to advocate the use of English to teach content courses (MoE, 2001), which inaugurated the process of EMI in China. Subsequently, MoE (2005, 2010) continued to stipulate more guidelines for bilingual education, predominantly Chinese-English bilingual education, to foster the growth of EMI. According to an MoE questionnaire survey on the state of bilingual education in higher education institutions (HEIs), 97.8% of universities launched bilingual courses, which meant there were 44 bilingual courses per HEI by April 2006 (Wang, 2019). Some top universities even offer around 200 EMI or bilingual courses (Tong et al., 2020).

Despite its rapid development, EMI is not without problems, which has attracted much research attention. Extant studies have examined a multitude of issues, including stakeholders' perceptions of and attitudes towards EMI (e.g. Macaro et al., 2018), impacts of EMI on content and language learning (e.g. Hu & Lei, 2014), misalignment of EMI envisioned goals and realities (e.g. Duran et al., 2022), EMI-related policymaking (e.g. Xu et al., 2021), EMI teacher professional development (e.g. Yuan, 2020), to name just a few, making EMI one of the hottest research topics in the academia. A prominent issue investigated in previous research concerns diverse stakeholders' subjectivity on EMI practice. However, previous research on subjectivity has relied primarily on questionnaires, interviews or focus groups (Graham & Eslami, 2019). There is thus a need for more innovative research methods to enhance our understandings of stakeholders' viewpoints. In this regard, Q methodology may prove to be a valuable approach for EMI studies.

Q methodology was first introduced by William Stephenson (1935) in the 1930s as a means of understanding subjectivity in the field of psychology. It has gained traction as an alternative research approach in the humanities and social sciences over the past few decades (Irie et al., 2018; Lundberg et al., 2020). In particular, it has been increasingly applied to investigate subjectivity in language education, including foreign language learners' enjoyment in online classes (Thumvichit, 2022), language learners' self-concept and motivation (Zheng et al., 2020), teachers' beliefs about engagement strategies for students (Yuan & Lo Bianco, 2022), perceptions of teacher competencies (Irie et al., 2018), teacher perceptions of educational multilingual reforms (Lundberg, 2019), language teachers' experiences of anxiety (Fraschini & Park, 2021) and various stakeholders' views on language policies (Slaughter et al., 2019). The accelerated use of Q methodology in language education research suggests that it may be a useful and valuable approach in EMI research as well.

However, despite its focus on complex issues and continuing interest in subjective perspectives, EMI research has been relatively slow to take up this approach. In this chapter, we seek to introduce Q methodology and diversify EMI research methods as advocated by Macaro et al. (2018). To that end, we first introduce Q methodology by focusing on its underlying philosophical and methodological assumptions. Then we detail the workflow of designing a Q study to help novice Q researchers get familiar with the methodology. Following that, we illustrate the methodology with a newly published research article on EMI (Deignan & Morton, 2022). Finally, we conclude this chapter by discussing its potential application in EMI research.

1.2 Q methodology

Q methodology includes a set of philosophical and epistemological underpinnings, data collection techniques, data analysis methods and factor interpretation strategies for the scientific study of subjectivity (Brown, 1993). Taking a person-centred rather than a variable-centred approach, it attempts to provide a holistic configuration of participants' subjectivity on complex issues and topics. In a nutshell, Q methodology involves a group of participants rank ordering a range of statements on a given topic. Participants instead of statements are then intercorrelated with each other. The resulting intercorrelations matrix is subjected to factor analysis to identify and cluster groups of participants with shared views on the topic. Finally, by recourse to various interpretation strategies, it constructs a narration grounded in the configuration and post-sorting interviews/surveys and offers a miniature of the view pool on the topic at hand.

Q methodology differs from traditional quantitative methodology in that it follows completely different philosophical and methodological premises (Brown, 1980). To begin with, Q methodology was developed to challenge the traditional quantitative scientific or hypothetico-deductive approach (Stephenson, 1936; Watts & Stenner, 2005). Unlike the hypothetico-deductive approach that aims at testing a hypothesis, Q methodology endeavours to generate an explanation and develop a theory (Brown, 1993). As such, Q is premised on non-positivist philosophies and epistemologies and can therefore be characterised as a qualitative method (Watts & Stenner, 2005, cf. Ramlo, 2016; Stenner & Stainton Rogers, 2004). Brown (1993, p. 130), for example, perceives it to be 'a useful addition to the qualitative researcher's arsenal'. As Rieber (2020, p. 2530) points out, even the highly statistical process of correlation and factor analysis in Q 'is guided by and dependent on qualitative decisions'.

Furthermore, Q focuses on 'participant-led subjective expressions and viewpoints' instead of 'researcher-led objective measurements' (Watts & Stenner, 2005, p. 69). For this reason, Q research allows participants to express their own subjectivities based on their own reference as opposed to any external metrics; it does not intend to extrapolate findings to a larger population; and participants in Q research are typically drawn purposively and the sample size is often small compared with that in survey research. Finally, Q research takes a holistic and hermeneutic approach to interpreting results from factor analysis and requires narrative accounts of the interpretation. These inherent features of Q methodology make it particularly suitable for exploring subjective and socially shared perspectives on complex and/or controversial issues.

1.3   Stages of Q research

In their systematic review of Q studies in education, Lundberg et al. (2020) identify a six-step process for Q methodological research: concourse development, Q set construction, participants' Q sorting, post-sorting activities, Q factor analysis and factor interpretation. These six steps can be synergised into three stages: (1) From concourse to Q set; (2) Q sorting and post-sorting activities; and (3) From Q factor analysis to factor interpretation.

1.3.1   Stage 1: from concourse to Q set

The first step in designing a Q study is to generate a concourse or a list of statements that reflect sufficiently all possible viewpoints on a given topic. The statements can come from different sources, including both naturalistic (e.g. interviews or questionnaire responses from participants) and ready-made sources (e.g. academic literature and newspapers) (McKeown & Thomas, 2013). They may come in different forms, such as statements, pictures and videos. The next step is to select a manageable, balanced and representative sample of statements from the concourse, which is referred to as a Q set or Q sample. Statements selected for the Q set are supposed to reflect the diversity and complexity of the subjectivities covered in the concourse. There are two main approaches to sampling statements for the Q set, including structured and unstructured sampling (McKeown & Thomas, 2013). The structured sampling approach selects statements from the concourse and divides them into subcategories systematically by drawing on existing theories, previous research or emergent themes from the initial statements. By contrast, the unstructured sampling approach does not draw on existing theories or previous research, nor does it split statements into categories. In this approach, researchers deduce an *ad hoc* framework from the Q concourse until no new viewpoints or statements can be added to the Q set. Q set is typically reviewed by experts and/or piloted with comparable participants to remove irrelevant, duplicate and unclear statements and to ensure that it not only captures the diverse views in the concourse but also includes as few statements as possible so as to reduce participants' burden in Q sorting.

1.3.2 Stage 2: Q sorting and post-sorting activities

Data collection in Q research often consists of Q sorting and post-sorting activities. Unlike quantitative approaches that often need large sample sizes, a Q study does not need a large sample size (typically no more than 40; Brown, 2003, p. 3). Thus, participants in a Q study, called a P set or P sample, are often drawn purposively, which is geared towards theoretical generalisability as opposed to statistical generalisability (Van Exel & Graaf, 2005). Convenient or snowball sampling is also acceptable, considering potential challenges in accessing certain participants. A rule of thumb is to select as diverse a P set as possible so that it represents the fullest possible range of subjectivities. In Q sorting, participants are asked to slot Q set into a Q grid by ranking statements relative to each other on a continuum (e.g. from 'disagree most' to 'agree most') and thus assigning meaning to each statement from their own standpoints. A Q grid is a quasi-normal distribution with a rating scale (e.g. -4 to $+4$, -5 to $+5$, or -6 to $+6$) across the top of the distribution (see Figure 1.1). The distribution and range of a Q grid depend on the number of statements and the controversy of the topic at hand (Van Exel & Graaf, 2005). If participants are expected to sort the Q set distinctly and clearly, it should be flatter so that more statements can be placed in extreme slots. On the contrary, if participants' perspectives are deemed ambiguous or inconclusive, the distribution of the Q grid should be steeper, providing more room in the middle of the Q grid. However, neither the distribution nor the range of the Q grid has any major impact on the results (Brown, 1980).

While there is no correct way to do Q sorting, participants are often asked to first divide the Q statements into three piles (e.g. disagree, neutral and

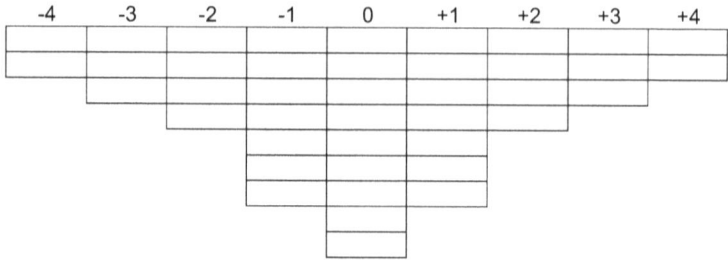

Figure 1.1 A typical Q-sort grid

agree) to make the sorting task easier. Therefore, they first read through the Q set and familiarise themselves with all Q statements involved. Following that, they sort these piles orderly into the Q grid, based on their comparison between different Q statements within the same pile. Q sorting can be conducted either face to face or online using such dedicated tools as Q-assessor (The Epimetrics Group, 2016), Q-sortware (Pruneddu & Zentner, 2011) or WebQ (Schmolck, 1999). After Q sorting, a post-sorting interview or a survey is often conducted to gather participants' demographics and rationales for their sorting. These additional materials are particularly valuable for subsequent interpretation (Watts & Stenner, 2012)

1.3.3   Stage 3: from Q factor analysis to factor interpretation

Data analysis in Q involves a process of data reduction that aims to compare and group participants' sorts into a few representative factors. Q methodology employs a by-person factor analysis, which inverts the conventional factor analysis by treating participants rather than statements as variables (Brown, 1993). Thus, while the statement configuration created by participants is inter-correlated and subjected to factor analysis, participants rather than statements are loaded on the extracted factors. This person-centred approach is designed to generate a holistic configuration of participants' views.

As with standard principal component analysis and factor analysis, factor analysis in Q also consists of two main steps: extraction and rotation (McKeown & Thomas, 2013; Watts & Stenner, 2012). Various dedicated software packages are available for analysing Q sorts, including PQMethod (Schmolck & Atkinson, 2014), qmethod for R (Zabala, 2014), PCQ program (Stricklin, 1996), and Ken-Q analysis (Banasick, 2018). There are two main approaches to extracting factors in Q factor analysis: centroid factor extraction and principal component analysis. While the former embraces indeterminacy and allows for more exploration of the data, the latter yields the best mathematical solution (Watts & Stenner, 2012). Eigenvalues greater than 1.00 and having at least two statistically significant Q sorts loading on a factor alone are two of the most frequently used criteria for deciding how many and which factors to retain (McKeown & Thomas, 2013; Watts & Stenner, 2012).

Factors thus extracted may be subjected to factor rotation, which repositions factors to simplify the structure of factors and thus facilitate their interpretation (Brown, 1980). There are also two prevalent methods of rotation: varimax and manual (Churruca et al., 2021; Lundberg et al., 2020). Varimax rotation is typically adopted to simplify the factor solution from a statistical point of view, whereas manual rotation is used to align with theoretical reasoning. After rotation, researchers need to decide which Q sorts should act as the exemplar of the factor, a process that is called flagging. This begins with an examination of factor loadings in the rotated matrix and then moves on to the division of Q sorts into three categories, those loaded significantly on only one factor (exemplar Q sorts), those loaded insignificantly on any factor (insignificant Q sorts) and those loaded significantly on more than one factor (confounded Q sorts). Confounded and insignificant sorts are typically excluded from subsequent analyses.

Factor interpretation in Q research is highly qualitative and holistic (Lundberg et al., 2020). It involves naming and describing each factor and summarising narrative accounts of extracted factors (factor arrays and factor scores). Specifically, the interpretation of factors in Q research relies on factor scores rather than factor loadings (Brown, 1993). A factor score is the average of scores for a Q statement given by all the participants (Q sorts) that significantly load on the factor. A factor array is created through this weighted averaging of all Q sorts significantly associated with each factor. The factor array is often presented in a table that includes both Q statements and factor scores for each Q statement. Three types of Q statements are of particular interest: characterising, consensus and distinguishing statements. Characterising statements are ranked extremely high or low in a factor, and they are often examined first at the interpretation stage (Watts & Stenner, 2012). While consensus statements refer to statements that are ranked similarly across factors, distinguishing statements are statements that are ranked differently across factors. The former highlights areas of agreement between perspectives, whereas the latter underscores areas of disagreement between them. To facilitate factor interpretation, researchers may also consult and examine post-sorting interviews and/or surveys.

1.4 An example study

Having sketched out the key stages of designing and conducting a Q study, we now present a sample study to illustrate its use in EMI research. Deignan and Morton (2022, p. 3) sought to unravel 'the complex, dynamic, and multidimensional nature of the use of EMI in HE [higher education]'. The study focused specifically on shared viewpoints on the challenges of EMI among

24 EMI subject lecturers. Drawing on activity theory and Q methodology, it identified three distinct shared perspectives, including favouring pedagogic integration of content and language, favouring 'English-only' EMI and having concerns about language and pedagogy. The results reported in the article focus on the third perspective with the methodological details and information on the other two viewpoints stored as supplementary materials on the IRIS database (www.iris-database.org/iris/app/home/index).

As the purpose of the study was to uncover shared perspectives on a complex issue—the challenges of EMI for subject lecturers, Q methodology was a suited approach. A Q concourse of 200 heterogeneous and relevant statements was developed through a review of the academic literature and communications with individuals who had experiences with EMI. Activity theory served as the theoretical framework for the derivation of Q set from the Q concourse, which indicates that the study utilised a structured sampling approach. According to activity theory (Engeström, 1987), seven constituent components were involved in the activity context of higher education internationalisation, including subject, tools, rules, community, division of labour, problem space and desired outcomes. Therefore, statements in the Q concourse were selected and allocated into these categories, producing a Q set of 48 statements.

The Q grid utilised a 7-point scale ranging from −3 (disagree most) to +3 (agree most). A P set of 24 EMI lecturers was drawn purposively from three state universities in Madrid that offered various EMI undergraduate and graduate programmes across a wide spectrum of disciplines. Probably due to the constraints of space, the study only mentioned the process of participants' rank-ordering statements and talking about their feelings without elaborating on the details about the Q sorting process. Following standard Q sorting procedures, the P set was supposed to first divide the Q set into three piles (positive, neutral and negative) and then rank order the Q sorts into the Q grid. Subsequent to the Q sorting, the P set would typically be interviewed about the rationale of their sorting, which would assist and/or corroborate future interpretation. However, little information about these procedures was reported either in the article or in the supplementary materials.

The Q sorts were analysed using Ken-Q Analysis, a dedicated web app for Q factor analysis. Principal component analysis and varimax rotation were employed to extract factors and produce a factor matrix (Table 1.2 in the Supplementary Materials of the sample study). Eight Q sorts were selected or flagged to form Factor 1, six to Factor 2 and another six to Factor 3. The study considered Q sorts with 0.6 and above loadings to be good candidates for a representative factor and those with 0.3 or below to be poor ones. By calculating the weighted average of the scores given to each statement by participants significantly loaded on each factor, an ideal Q sort—that 'represents how a hypothetical respondent with a 100% loading on that factor would have ordered all the statements of the Q-set' (Van Exel & Graaf, 2005, p. 9)—was produced. The ideal Q sort was then converted into a factor array within the app, which would help identify consensus and distinguishing statements to facilitate interpretation. Drawing on consensus statements, the study briefly discussed viewpoints shared across the three factors, which shed light on the viewpoints of all the EMI lecturers in the current study. With reference to distinguishing statements, the boundaries between the three factors were delineated. As noted earlier, the study reported in the article focused primarily on Factor 3. The most salient issue that emerged in Factor 3 concerned the relations between language and pedagogy. Participants with shared views on this factor held that language may influence the achievement of pedagogical goals, as typified by the statement ranked at +2 below.

6. EMI can inhibit a teacher's personality and teaching style, limiting interaction and the possibilities for building rapport with students. (+2) (Supplementary Materials of the sample study, p. 6)

Apart from these distinguishing statements, Factor 3 also converged on the perceived benefits of EMI to lecturers, students and universities, which rendered it pro-EMI. Thus, Factor 3 was labelled as pro-EMI despite concerns about language and pedagogy.

1.5 Conclusion

This chapter is intended to serve as a primer on Q methodology in EMI research. It has discussed its underlying assumptions and outlined its major stages. An example study has been presented to illustrate its application in EMI research. Q methodology has several advantages that distinguish it from other approaches. First, participants rely on self-reference in Q sorting and can thus fully express their opinions without a priori influence from researchers. Second, compared with survey research, only a small number of participants are needed for a Q study, which makes it cost-efficient and manageable for many researchers. Third, Q seeks to uncover the range of subjective and socially shared views, which makes it possible for all voices to be heard, including ones that are often marginalised by other approaches (Brown, 2006). Last but not least, thanks to the development of dedicated software packages and web-based apps, Q sorting and data analysis have become increasingly easier.

EMI researchers have shown time-honoured interest in stakeholders' perspectives on various issues, such as attitudes, beliefs, motivations and perceptions (Graham & Eslami, 2019; Macaro et al., 2018). As Macaro et al. (2018, p. 64) have observed, 'EMI in HE research is dominated by research questions relating to teacher and/or student beliefs, perceptions and attitudes towards its introduction and practice'. A wide range of research methods have been applied to explore these issues, including questionnaires, interviews and focus groups, among others (Lei & Hu, 2022; Tong et al., 2020). Nonetheless, to better understand the complex and dynamic nature of EMI, we need to expand our research methodology repertoire (Macaro et al., 2018). To the best of our knowledge, only two published studies (Deignan & Morton, 2022; Gyenes, 2021) have tapped on the potential of Q for EMI research. The example study presented here shows that Q methodology is a viable approach to enhancing our understanding of subject lecturers' perceptions of challenges in EMI.

Additionally, and relatedly, Q has the potential to offer glimpses into stakeholders' beliefs about (dis)advantages of different EMI models (Curle et al., 2020), attitudes towards different varieties of English in EMI programmes (Coleman, 2006), views on the role of the first language in EMI (Graham & Eslami, 2019) and the functions of English in cultural identity and the status of other languages in science (Coleman, 2006). Moreover, Q can also be applied to uncover stakeholders' motivations for implementing or partaking in EMI programmes (Macaro et al., 2018) and differences and similarities in the motivations of stakeholders from different backgrounds (e.g. male vs. female and private vs. public schools) (Lei & Hu, 2022). Furthermore, Q can help further our knowledge of stakeholders' perspectives on EMI policies. Researchers can draw on Q methodology to explore support systems various stakeholders need (Macaro et al., 2018; Tong et al., 2020) and identify possible gaps between policy envisions and ground realities (Aizawa & Rose, 2019; Hu & Lei, 2014; Hu et al., 2014). Finally, identity construction in EMI can also benefit from the use of Q. Although identity has been rarely examined in EMI (Tong et al., 2020), issues related to it are expected to affect the quality of EMI and thus deserve our research attention. Q constitutes a promising approach for investigating these and many other issues related to EMI.

References

Aizawa, I., & Rose, H. (2019). An analysis of Japan's English as medium of instruction initiatives within higher education: The gap between meso-level policy and micro-level practice. *Higher Education, 77*(6), 1125–1142. https://doi.org/10.1007/s10734-018-0323-5

Banasick, S. (2018). *Ken-Q analysis: A web application for Q methodology* (0.11.1). https://shawnbanasick.github.io/ken-q-analysis-beta/index.html#section1

Brown, S. R. (1980). *Political subjectivity: Applications of Q methodology in political science*. Yale University Press.

Brown, S. R. (1993). A primer on Q methodology. *Operant Subjectivity, 16*(3/4), 91–138.

Brown, S. R. (2003). *Empowerment as subjective operant*. Workshop on "Measuring Empowerment: Cross-Disciplinary Perspectives" held at the World Bank in Washington, DC, on February, 4.

Brown, S. R. (2006). A match made in heaven: A marginalized methodology for studying the marginalized. *Quality & Quantity, 40*, 361–382

Churruca, K., Ludlow, K., Wu, W., Gibbons, K., Nguyen, H. M., Ellis, L. A., & Braithwaite, J. (2021). A scoping review of Q-methodology in healthcare research. *BMC*

Medical Research Methodology, 21(1), 125. https://doi.org/10.1186/s12874-021-01309-7

Coleman, J. A. (2006). English-medium teaching in European higher education. *Language Teaching, 39*(1), 1–14. https://doi.org/10.1017/S026144480600320X

Curle, S., Jablonkai, R., Mittelmeier, J., Sahan, K., & Veitch, A. (2020). English medium part 1: Literature review. In N. Galloway (Ed.), *English in higher education* (Report No. 978-0-86355-977-8). British Council.

Deignan, T., & Morton, T. (2022). The challenges of English medium instruction for subject lecturers: A shared viewpoint. *ELT Journal, 76*(2), 208–217. https://doi.org/10.1093/elt/ccab084

Duran, D., Kurhila, S., & Sert, O. (2022). Word search sequences in teacher-student interaction in an English as medium of instruction context. *International Journal of Bilingual Education and Bilingualism, 25*(2), 502–521. https://doi.org/10.1080/13670050.2019.1703896

Engeström, Y. (1987). *Learning by expanding*. Orienta-Konsultit Oy.

The Epimetrics Group. (2016). *Q-Assessor*. www.q-assessor.com

Fraschini, N., & Park, H. (2021). Anxiety in language teachers: Exploring the variety of perceptions with Q methodology. *Foreign Language Annals, 54*(2), 341–364. https://doi.org/10.1111/flan.12527

Graham, K. M., & Eslami, Z. R. (2019). Attitudes toward EMI in East Asia and the gulf: A systematic review. *Language Problems & Language Planning, 43*(1), 8–31. https://doi.org/10.1075/lplp.00030.gra

Gyenes, A. (2021). Student perceptions of critical thinking in EMI programs at Japanese universities: A Q-methodology study. *Journal of English for Academic Purposes, 54*, 20. https://doi.org/10.1016/j.jeap.2021.101053

Hu, G., & Lei, J. (2014). English-medium instruction in Chinese higher education: A case study. *Higher Education, 67*(5), 551–567. https://doi.org/10.1007/s10734-013-9661-5

Hu, G., Li, L., & Lei, J. (2014). English-medium instruction at a Chinese University: Rhetoric and reality. *Language Policy, 13*(1), 21–40. https://doi.org/10.1007/s10993-013-9298-3

Irie, K., Ryan, S., & Mercer, S. (2018). Using Q methodology to investigate pre-service EFL teachers' mindsets about teaching competences. *Studies in Second Language Learning and Teaching, 8*(3), 575–598. https://doi.org/10.14746/ssllt.2018.8.3.3

Lei, J., & Hu, G. (2022). Research on English-medium instruction in the Asia Pacific: Trends, foci, challenges, and strategies. In O. Lee, P. Brown, A. L. Goodwin, & A. Green (Eds.), *International handbook on education development in Asia-Pacific* (pp. 1–23). Springer. https://doi.org/10.1007/978-981-16-2327-1_23-1

Lundberg, A. (2019). Teachers' beliefs about multilingualism: Findings from Q method research. *Current Issues in Language Planning, 20*(3), 266–283.

Lundberg, A., de Leeuw, R., & Aliani, R. (2020). Using Q methodology: Sorting out subjectivity in educational research. *Educational Research Review, 31*, 100361. https://doi.org/10.1016/j.edurev.2020.100361

Macaro, E., Curle, S., Pun, J., An, J., & Dearden, J. (2018). A systematic review of English medium instruction in higher education. *Language Teaching, 51*(1), 36–76. https://doi.org/10.1017/S0261444817000350

McKeown, B., & Thomas, D. B. (2013). *Q methodology* (Vol. 66). Sage.

Ministry of Education. (2001). *Recommendations on strengthening college undergraduate programmes and enhancing the quality of instruction.* http://old.moe.gov.cn//publicfiles/business/htmlfiles/moe/moe_18/200108/241.html

Ministry of Education. (2005). *Recommendations on further strengthening undergraduate programmes and the quality of instruction.* http://old.moe.gov.cn//publicfiles/business/htmlfiles/moe/moe_18/200108/241.html

Ministry of Education. (2010). *The notice of 2010 bilingual demonstration course project.* http://old.moe.gov.cn/publicfiles/business/htmlfiles/moe/s3850/201008/93899.html

Pruneddu, A., & Zentner, M. (2011). The "Q-sortware" as a web tool for personality assessment. *Poster presented at the 27th annual Q conference*, Birmingham, UK.

Ramlo, S. (2016). Mixed method lessons learned from 80 years of Q methodology. *Journal of Mixed Methods Research, 10*(1), 28–45. https://doi.org/10.1177/1558689815610998

Rieber, L. P. (2020). Q methodology in learning, design, and technology: An introduction. *Educational Technology Research and Development, 68*(5), 2529–2549. https://doi.org/10.1007/s11423-020-09777-2

Schmolck, P. (1999). *WebQ q-sorting over the net.* http://schmolck.org/qmethod/webq/

Schmolck, P., & Atkinson, J. (2014). *PQMethod*, version 2.35. http://schmolck.userweb.mwn.de/qmethod/

Slaughter, Y., Bianco, J. L., Aliani, R., Cross, R., & Hajek, J. (2019). Language programming in rural and regional Victoria: Making space for local viewpoints in policy development. *Australian Review of Applied Linguistics, 42*(3), 274–300. https://doi.org/10.1075/aral.18030.sla

Stenner, P., & Stainton Rogers, R. (2004). Q methodology and qualiquantology: The example of discriminating between emotions. In Z. Todd, B. Nerlich, S. McKeown, & D. D. Clarke (Eds.), *Mixing methods in psychology: The integration of qualitative and quantitative methods in theory and practice* (pp. 101–117). Psychology Press.

Stephenson, W. (1935). Technique of factor analysis. *Nature, 136*(3434), 297–297. https://doi.org/10.1038/136297b0

Stephenson, W. (1936). The inverted factor technique. *British Journal of Psychology, 26*, 344–361.

Stricklin, M. (1996). *PCQ: Factor analysis program for Q-technique* (Version 3.8). Stricklin, M.

Thumvichit, A. (2022). Unfolding the subjectivity of foreign language enjoyment in online classes: A Q methodology study. *Journal of Multilingual and Multicultural Development*, 1–18. https://doi.org/10.1080/01434632.2022.2050917

Tong, F. H., Wang, Z. Y., Min, Y., & Tang, S. F. (2020). A systematic literature synthesis of 19 years of bilingual education in Chinese higher education: Where does the academic discourse stand? *Sage Open, 10*(2), 23. https://doi.org/10.1177/2158244020926510

Van Exel, J., & De Graaf, G. (2005). *Q methodology: A sneak preview.* www.researchgate.net/publication/228574836_Q_Methodology_A_Sneak_Preview

Wang, Y. (2019). The role of English in the internalization of Chinese higher education a case study of English-medium instruction in China. In Kumiko Murata (Ed.), *English medium instruction from an English as a lingua franca perspective: Exploring the higher education context* (pp. 201–218). Routledge.

Watts, S., & Stenner, P. (2005). Doing Q methodology: Theory, method and interpretation. *Qualitative Research in Psychology*, *2*(1), 67–91. https://doi.org/10.1191/1478088705qp022oa

Watts, S., & Stenner, P. (2012). *Doing Q methodological research: Theory, method and interpretation*. Sage.

Xu, X., Rose, H., McKinley, J., & Zhou, S. H. (2021). The incentivisation of English medium instruction in Chinese universities: Policy misfires and misalignments. *Applied Linguistics Review*, *23*. https://doi.org/10.1515/applirev-2021-0181

Yuan, C., & Lo Bianco, J. (2022). L2 Chinese teachers' beliefs about engagement strategies for students in Australia: Findings from Q methodology research. *System*, *106*, 102792. https://doi.org/10.1016/j.system.2022.102792

Yuan, R. (2020). Promoting EMI teacher development in EFL higher education contexts: A teacher educator's reflections. *RELC Journal*, *51*(2), 309–317. https://doi.org/10.1177/0033688219878886

Zabala, A. (2014). qmethod: A package to explore human perspectives using Q methodology. *The R Journal*, *6*(2), 163–173. https://journal.r-project.org/archive/2014-2/zabala.pdf

Zheng, Y., Lu, X., & Ren, W. (2020). Tracking the evolution of Chinese learners' multilingual motivation through a longitudinal Q methodology. *The Modern Language Journal*, *104*(4), 781–803. https://doi.org/10.1111/modl.12672

2 How to conduct a multimodal classroom discourse analysis

Fei Victor Lim

2.1 Multimodal classroom discourse analysis

The interaction between the teacher and students has intrigued education researchers for almost a century (Christie, 1993; Kress et al., 2005; Lim, 2021a, Mercer, 2000; Sinclair & Coulthard, 1975; Walsh, 2006; Weninger et al., forthcoming). Sinclair and Coulthard (1975) reflect that an interest in classroom language studies started in the 1940s and research into many areas of discourse, including classroom discourse, has been undertaken since.

These pedagogic interactions are often analysed in a bid to understand the nature of teaching and learning in the classroom. The focus of the analysis could be on the instructional discourse, that is the discourse on 'transmitting specialised competencies', and regulative discourse, that is the discourse on 'creating specialised order, relation and identity' in pedagogic discourse (Bernstein, 1990, p. 183). The former is about the knowledge and content taught, and the latter, the dynamics of interpersonal social relations between the teacher and the student in the pedagogic interaction.

Before the mass accessibility and affordability of video recording technologies, classroom research tended to revolve around the collection and analysis of audio recordings, often triangulated by the researcher's field notes during the lesson observation. As such, the focus tended to be on the words used by the teacher and the students during the lesson. One of the more popular approaches to classroom discourse analysis is Bellack et al. (1966)'s three-part exchange: Initiation, Response, Feedback (IRF). This IRF exchange is more famously extended by Sinclair and Coulthard (1975). The same phenomenon is observed by Mehan (1979), who described it as the Initiation, Response, Evaluation (IRE) sequence. It has been touted by Edwards and Westgate (1994) as being 'the essential teaching exchange' (p. 124). However, the usefulness of the IRF sequences has also been challenged in several studies (Mercer, 2007), such as assuming a 'stimulus/response progression to classroom discourse' (Walsh, 2006, p. 40) as well as relying on a sole focus on language to understand the pedagogic interaction (Lim, 2011, 2019, 2021a, 2021b).

DOI: 10.4324/9781003375531-3

The meanings made in the classroom are expressed not just with words alone but multimodally, through the teacher's gestures (Lim, 2019, 2021b), gaze (Amundrud, 2018), as well as positioning and movement in the classroom space (Kress et al., 2005; Lim et al., 2012). As such, the focus on words alone offers an impoverished understanding of the pedagogic discourse. The 'multimodal turn' in education (Jewitt, 2009) entails a recognition that teaching and learning involve the teacher's multimodal orchestration of meaning-making resources (Jewitt, 2008). Lim (2021a) describes the use of a full range of semiotic resources in the design of students' learning experiences as embodied teaching. The increasingly common use of video recording technologies in education research now allows for the teacher' use of gestures, gaze, positioning and movement as well as other multimodal orchestration to be recorded in tandem with speech. The video data collected thus demand analytical approaches that can attend to the multimodal meanings made in the pedagogic discourse.

While beginning with an interest in language, scholars in the field of conversation analysis (CA) have also included the use of gestures that accompany speech in interactions (Goodwin, 1979; Schegloff, 1984; Ochs et al., 1996). Mondada (2016) reflects that, within the field of CA, the growing inclusion of embodied resources beyond speech can be situated 'within a more global and holistic approach of multimodality, comprising language, gesture, gaze, head movements, facial expressions, body posture, body movements, and embodied manipulations of material objects' (p. 338). CA approaches offer education researchers a way to attend to the interaction patterns emerging from the multimodal classroom data rather than relying on any preconceived systems (Seedhouse, 2004). Notwithstanding, given the lack of preconceived categories proposed, Walsh (2006) suggests that the CA approach to classroom discourse may also be seen as 'whimsical or idealised to illustrate particular points' (p. 54). Lim (2021b) observes that conversational analysis approaches tend to focus on the 'multimodal semantics' level rather than the 'multimodal grammatics' level where the interplay of semiotic resources at the granular level is examined (p. 38).

Such attention to the orchestration of multimodal resources is from researchers adopting a multimodal approach, rather than a 'Linguistics-Plus' approach (Jewitt et al., 2021), to classroom discourse analysis. Jewitt et al. (2016) state that a multimodal study is where 'multimodality is central to aims, research questions, theory and method' rather than in which multimodal concepts are 'used selectively' (p. 5). One feature of multimodal discourse analysis is its fine-grained examination of the specific choices and meanings made (Flewitt, 2006).

Multimodal approaches to classroom discourse analysis have been increasingly undertaken by researchers in recent years (e.g. Boistrup & Selander, 2022; Diamantopoulou & Orevik, 2021; Kress et al., 2021; Lim, 2021a; Takahashi & Yu, 2017). In this chapter, I will outline an approach informed by systemic functional theory (Halliday, 1975) for the multimodal classroom discourse analysis. The Systemic Functional Multimodal Discourse Analysis (SFMDA) approach (O'Halloran & Lim, 2014) is concerned with the 'grammatics', that is the 'functions of different semiotic resources and the meanings that arise when semiotic choices combine in multimodal phenomena' (Jewitt et al., 2016, p. 30). SFMDA focuses on examining the semiotic choices and the metafunctions they serve in the multimodal discourse. The metafunctions, following systemic functional theory, are described in terms of the ideational meaning, that is the represented ideas and experiences, the interpersonal meaning, that is the constructed social relations between the participants, and the textual meaning, that is the organisation of the message.

In the next section, I will describe an example of a classroom discourse analysis based on the SFMDA approach and discuss the methodological considerations in examining the multimodal data from this theoretical orientation. Following this, I will reflect on the lessons learnt and the value of the approach as well as the challenges and the limitations of the SFMDA approach. The goal is to inspire other education researchers towards applying the SFMDA approach to classroom discourse analysis with a clear understanding of its affordances and constraints as a qualitative research method.

2.2 SFMDA approach to classroom discourse analysis

2.2.1 Theoretical frameworks

This case study is drawn from my research project on how a language teacher, with more than 10 years of teaching experience, in an English-medium instruction (EMI) classroom in a junior college (pre-university level) in Singapore, designs the learning experience of her students through her embodied teaching during the lesson. In recognition that 'how teachers and students use gaze, body posture, and the distribution of space and resources produces silent discourses in the classroom that affect literacy' (Jewitt, 2008, p. 262), I wanted to extend the scope of my study beyond the teacher's use of speech to cover her multimodal orchestration of semiotic resources, including her gestures as well as her positioning and movement in the classroom. I was interested in understanding the specific meanings that could be made with these semiotic resources in expressing the instructional and regulative discourses during the lesson. I also wanted to understand the interplay of the semiotic resources in the teacher's embodied teaching during the lesson in contributing to the students' learning experience.

The case study is described in detail in Lim (2011, 2021a), and the focus in this chapter is on offering a more reflective stance on the methodological decisions made in the research process. The study was guided by a broad question that seeks to elucidate the nature of the teacher's multimodal orchestration in her pedagogy. This necessitates research methods that offer conceptual frameworks and tools to both analyse the meanings made in the specific use of semiotic resources in a granular manner as well as having a shared set of principles to discuss the interplay of meanings across speech, gestures, positioning and movement.

As such, I applied a multimodal discourse analysis approach that is informed by systemic functional theory to analyse the video data of the teacher' embodied teaching I collected. The SFMDA approach (O'Halloran & Lim, 2014), as described earlier, is based on the principle of the metafunctional organisation of meaning. While Halliday (1994) first developed systemic functional grammar to map the meanings made in language across the metafunctions with systems such as transitivity in language to realise ideational meaning, mood and modality to realise interpersonal meaning, and information valuation to realise textual meaning, other researchers have subsequently applied the metafunctional principle to map the meanings in other semiotic resources as well. Most famously, Kress and van Leeuwen (1996) developed visual grammar as a conceptual framework organised metafunctionally to describe the meanings made in images. O'Toole (1994) has also applied the metafunctional principle to examine the meanings made in paintings, sculptures and architecture. The teacher's linguistic choices are thus analysed with systemic functional grammar in my research study and the other semiotic resources with frameworks and conceptions that share the metafunctional principle and informed by systemic functional theory as well.

In relation to the study of embodied semiotic resources from the systemic functional theoretical perspective, Martinec (2000, 2001) developed a system for actions and Hood (2007) conceptualised the meanings of gestures in terms of the ideational, interpersonal and textual meaning made. For example, the ideational meaning in communicative gestures was described in terms of the functional semantic categorisation (Hood, 2007) as congruent entities, which could denote objects, and metaphorical concepts, which could connote abstract ideas. The ideational meaning in communicative gestures could also be expressed with hands out and open palms to signify receptivity. The interpersonal meaning in communicative gestures could encompass the nature of attitude, engagement and graduation. For example, an open-palm gesture could express engagement by signifying an expansion of 'heteroglossic space, inviting student voices into the discourse' (Hood, 2011, p. 46). Likewise, graduation could be expressed through the speed of the gesture. Slow moves could connote emphasis and deliberateness, while fast moves could convey a sense of urgency, energy and dynamism. The textual meaning in communicative gestures could be expressed through the act of pointing. Directionality and specificity could be communicated with pointing, with specificity at its highest degree when conveyed by the 'smallest body part . . . the little finger' (Hood, 2011, p. 38). The teacher could relate speech with visuals on the whiteboard or direct her words to a specific student. The act of pointing could also function interpersonally as an imperative to demand engagement. Drawing from their work, I examined the gestures used by the teacher during the lesson in terms of forms and functions they realised (Lim, 2019). Given the interest in SFMDA in the interplay of meanings in the multimodal ensemble, I drew from the work of O'Halloran (2005) and Royce (1998, 2006) on 'intersemiotic complementarity', Baldry and Thibault's (2006) 'resource integration principle', as well as Liu and O'Halloran's (2009) conceptualisation of image–language relations to theorise the intersemiosis between speech and gestures based on their contextualising relations (Lim, 2021b). The concepts of intersemiotic parallelism and intersemiotic polysemy were used to describe the interplay of meanings in the teacher's speech and gestures to reinforce the emergent meanings in the former and express 'new semantic layers of sarcasm or ambivalence' (Lim, 2021b, p. 50) in the latter.

For the analysis of the teacher's use of positioning and movement in the classroom, I was unable to find existing work in mapping the meaning of classroom spaces from the systemic functional theoretical perspectives. As such, I drew from the work of cultural anthropologist Edward Hall, who developed the concept of proxemics. He identified four general sets of space— namely public, social–consultative, casual-personal and intimate. This is based on the typical distances in which such interactions occur, as well as the extent of visibility and contact experienced by the other party (Hall, 1966). I located the socio-consultative space as the space where most of the positioning and movement of the teacher is made and sought to theorise the metafunctional meanings made in this space. For this, I drew on the work of Stenglin (2009), who examined the meanings of spaces in museums and parks from the metafunctional perspective as well as Kress et al.'s (2005) proposal that the meanings in classroom spaces are realised through the interaction of the teacher's movement; the meaning of the space in which the teacher moves, and how and where the students may move. For example, the meanings in the space can be reconfigured 'by the placement of the teacher's desk in relation to the rows of tables; and produced by the transforming action of the teacher in his pacing' (Kress et al., 2005, p. 26). Following these theoretical conceptions, I proposed a framework to describe the meanings in classroom spaces produced and transformed by the teacher's positioning in relation to the students and movement during the lesson (Lim et al., 2012). The spatial pedagogy framework offered me a way to analyse the teacher's use of space in the design of the learning experience and the shared metafunctional principles in which the meanings are mapped allowed me to discuss the interplay of meanings made in the teacher's multimodal pedagogy.

2.2.2 *Research planning and design*

In order to collect data from the classroom, issues of ethics and permissions following the requirements from the institutional review board need to be addressed. With the consent of the school and the head of the English department, we invited teachers to participate in the research study on a voluntary basis. As my research aim was to understand how a teacher designed a language learning experience for the students through her embodied teaching, I requested the participating teacher not to make special preparations for the lesson or to do anything out of the ordinary from the regular lessons they typically have with the students. It was also emphasised that while there will be discussions on the pedagogies adopted, the purpose is not to evaluate or assess her teaching ability. The teacher was also assured that she will remain anonymous in the subsequent dissemination of the findings.

As part of contextualising the multimodal discourse analysis, I also collected the curriculum documents and lesson materials from the teacher. As I formerly taught the subject in the school, my insider knowledge was helpful in offering me a more nuanced understanding of the nature of the subject, ways it can be taught as well as the profile of students in the junior college, now my site of study. Complementing this awareness, I also applied Christie's (2002) curriculum genre theory and O'Halloran's (2004) proposal of lesson microgenres to situate the segment of the lesson identified for close multimodal analysis. The curriculum genre theory is used to describe the levels of contextualisation from text to context, explain the translation of the subject from policy and curriculum documents to its instantiation as practice in the classroom and offer a basis on which the selection of texts for delicate analysis and cross-comparison can be made. O'Halloran (2004) extends the curriculum genre theory to examine the sequence of lesson stages, termed 'microgenres', which make up the lesson. The application of these theoretical conceptions enabled me to situate the fine-grained multimodal analysis within the context which it is situated in and allows me to zoom out from the detailed analysis and relate it to the lesson stage, the lesson, the curriculum, the subject disciplinarity as well as the education system with its values and philosophies. This is because one distinctiveness of the SFMDA approach is the granular examination of the semiotic choices made to express metafunctional meanings from the multimodal orchestration in the discourse. As such, the researcher may wish to offer a detailed discussion of the instances of meanings made during specific lesson stages. The curriculum genre theory and lesson microgenres (Lim, 2021a) thus allow the researcher to go deep into multimodal analysis without losing the context in which the discourse is situated.

Having made decisions on the theoretical framework and methodological approach, the next step is to consider how the data can be collected. As mentioned earlier, video recording technology is now easily available and is often used as the primary tool of data collection in classroom research. Video-recording can not only preserve 'the temporal and sequential structure which is so characteristic of interaction' (Knoblauch et al., 2009, p. 19) but also allow the researcher analyst to review the video sequence 'several times, with sound, without sound, in real-time, slow motion and fast forward' (Flewitt,

2006, p. 28). However, it must be recognised that video-recording offers only a partial view of the lesson experienced by the teacher. Depending on the availability of resources and research questions, the researcher may have to make decisions on whether to train the video camera on the teacher or the students. Even with two cameras, one focusing on the teacher and the other on the students, there may be times in which the students are organised into small groups for discussion, and decisions will have to be made by the researcher on which group to have the camera on. Ultimately, these decisions are to be guided by the research questions of the study and trade-offs will often have to be made on the data that can be collected. The nature of data collected is factored against 'more practical questions such as how much time and resource are available' (Jewitt et al., 2016, pp. 142–143).

2.2.3 Analysis

The analysis of the data begins with making decisions on how the video data should be transcribed and visualised. As Bezemer and Mavers (2011) observe, 'in representing social interaction in transcripts, "translations" are constantly made' and it is 're-making video as a multimodal transcript that researchers come to see differently' (p. 196). As such, transcription of the multimodal data, while seemingly technical in nature, must be recognised as an initial and integral part of the discourse analysis (Baldry & Thibault, 2006) as it is 'semiotic work' (Kress, 2010) and relies on the agency of the researcher in framing, selecting and highlighting the data.

The transcription of the video data will support both the macro analysis and micro analysis to be performed within the SFMDA approach (Lim & O'Halloran, 2012). In relation to macro analytical transcription, Baldry and Thibault (2006) explain that 'transcription is a way of revealing both the co-deployment of semiotic resources and their dynamic unfolding in time along textually constrained and enabled pathways or trajectories' (p. xvi). The purpose of the macro analysis is to surface patterns of meanings in the multimodal discourse. Specifically, in applying the SFMDA approach to examine the teacher's embodied teaching in this study, the macro analysis will show how the teacher uses language, gestures, as well as positioning and movement during the lesson to express the ideational, interpersonal and textual meanings. For example, in my study, it was observed that the teacher designed for 'structured informality' (Lim, 2021a) through the interpersonal meaning made in her semiotic choices to reduce hierarchical distance with the adolescent students in the learning, while maintaining a didactic structure in her lesson. In terms of the regulative discourse, the teacher used gestures and language to express the interpersonal meaning of relatability and informality to encourage the students' response and participation in her lesson. However, the interpersonal meaning of hierarchical power was asserted through her use of authoritative spaces in the classroom. The ideational meaning of structure and logical sequencing of information in her instructional discourse were expressed through her speech.

The micro analysis focused on the detailed examination of the semiotic choices made in selected segments of the multimodal discourse. In applying the SFMDA approach to examine the teacher's embodied teaching in this study, the micro analysis can be focused on specific lesson microgenres, such as the teacher's discourse on skills, content or discipline (the full suite of lesson microgenres in the English Language classroom is discussed in Lim, 2021a) to examine the role of the teacher's speech, gestures, as well as positioning and movement in expressing the metafunctional meanings in the multimodal discourse. For example, the micro analysis could reveal that the teacher tends to use her gestures, positioning and movement, rather than speech, to express the discourse of discipline. This could be observed in her semiotic choices to point at or move towards, rather than to scold, a distracted student during the lesson. As such the regulative discourse is expressed more with gestures as well as positioning and movement, and less with speech, in her embodied teaching pedagogy.

The macro and micro analytical transcription can be supported with technologies which offer a platform for the multimodal transcription of the dynamic video data. For example, video analysis software programs include the Multimodal Analysis Video (MMAV) developed by O'Halloran et al. (2012), the EUDICO Linguistic Annotator (ELAN) developed by Max Planck Institute for Psycholinguistics (Wittenburg et al., 2006) or the MAXQDA, a programme for the qualitative analysis of multimedia developed by VERBI Software (Kuckartz & Radiker, 2019). Some of these platforms, like ELAN, are freely available as open-source software, while others, like MMAV and MAXQDA, come with a price and with technical support. These platforms are comparable in their functionalities, with some, like MMAV, offering a more integrative experience, and the researcher could decide which platform best meets the needs of the study. In addition to supporting the transcription of the multimodal data, platforms, like the MMAV, also offer visualisation of the analysis with networked graphs. For example, the teacher's positioning and movement during the lesson can be visualised with the use of shapes, the duration of positioning and frequency of movement with sizes, and the directionality of the teacher's movement from one space to the next with arrows, with the use of colour and thickness of arrows to indicate frequency. Such visualisation supports the analysis of a large multimodal corpus and can allow the researcher to identify patterns as well as compare and contrast across the semiotic choices with greater ease.

Following the analysis of the data, the researcher will then offer an interpretation of the findings, which are supported by the textual evidence. Iedema (2001) reminds us that multimodal discourse analysis is 'an interpretative exercise, and not a search for "scientific proof"' (p. 198). Here the researcher is encouraged to draw on his life experience, knowledge of the field, and familiarity with the context, to make sense of the patterns of meanings that have emerged from the analysis, for example, the teacher's expression of a 'structured informality' through her embodied teaching. Structured informality is constructed through the interplay of multimodal meanings resulted from the effective combination of semiotic resources (Lim, 2021a). This interpretation was built on Vygotsky's (1978) conceptualisation of social constructivism in teaching and learning and extended by Savery and Duffy (1995), who argued that a teacher should structure the learning experience just enough to make sure that the students get clear guidance and parameters within which to achieve the learning objectives. However, the learning experience should be open and free enough to allow the students to discover, enjoy, interact and arrive at their own understanding and construction of knowledge. My past experience as a language teacher in the EMI classroom and my familiarity with the adolescent students in the school also contributed to my interpretation of the semiotic choices in the teacher's multimodal orchestration.

2.3 Challenges and opportunities

In this section, I discuss the challenges and the limitations of the SFMDA approach to classroom discourse analysis introduced in this chapter. I also reflect on how these issues can be addressed, mitigated, and overcome by drawing on the lessons I learnt from the research study as well as from the recent development in multimodal studies.

The first issue is theoretical. The frameworks for the analysis of language, gestures and space in the SFMDA approach were either based directly or built on the work of scholars working within the systemic functional theoretical paradigm. As Ochs (1979) notably argues, there is no theory-neutral analysis or transcription practices as the analytical approaches are always shaped by theory. It is therefore important to recognise that the theoretical lenses we apply may not only allow us to 'see' some aspects of social phenomenon better but also blind us to other aspects of the same phenomenon. For example, a criticism of SFMDA is whether the notion of a 'grammar' derived from language can similarly be applied to other semiotic resources, such as images, gestures and the use of space (Bateman, 2014). The tri-metafunctional organisation of meanings in discourse has also been subjected to challenge, with scholars such as Cope and Kalantzis (2020) proposing five functions of meaning, which include context and interest to the metafunctions. While each theoretical framework brings affordances and constraints, this challenge can be addressed by the researcher having a self-reflexive awareness of what the theoretical positioning offers and inhibits.

The second issue relates to the nature of multimodal data, being large and multi-faceted, which necessitates a 'laborious' analysis that can take 'a lot of time and concentration' (Iedema, 2001, p. 200). The fine-grained analysis distinctive of the SFMDA approach to classroom discourse is necessary to examine the interplay of semiotic choices and pays off when patterns of meanings are revealed and deeper insights into the instances of multimodal orchestration are identified. Trade-offs will often have to be made between the depth of analysis with the scope of the data. It is helpful to remember that the goal of multimodal discourse analysis is not seeking generalisability or representativeness. Rather, the goal is often consciousness-raising and to inform social action (Lemke, 1995; Iedema, 2001). Notwithstanding, the use of technological platforms, as introduced earlier, can alleviate some of the labour in the multimodal discourse analysis. Advances in multimodal analysis hold the promise of making multimodal discourse analysis less reliant on manual labour. These advances include automated analysis (Bateman & Hiippala, 2021; Hiippala, 2021), which involves integrating multimodal frameworks with computational models for big data, natural language processing, video processing and contextual metadata to develop powerful analytical and visualisation tools (O'Halloran et al., 2021).

The third issue stems from the centrality of the researcher in the analysis and the interpretational sense-making process in multimodal discourse analysis. As discussed earlier, the analysis and the interpretation could be supported or constrained by the background, training and astuteness of the researcher to identify the meanings and patterns of meanings made. While this may be true of all discourse analysis, it is exacerbated in multimodal discourse analysis, especially with embodied semiotic resources, such as gestures, where the meanings are less codified than language (Weninger et al., forthcoming). Hiippala (2021) reflects that 'humans excel in making situated discourse interpretations, draw on their embodied world knowledge and effortlessly update their inferences through abductive reasoning as additional evidence becomes available' (p. 138). A way to strengthen the reliability of the analysis and interpretation is to use inter-raters to analyse a sample of the data and measure the agreement between the analysts (Bateman et al., 2017; Bateman & Hiippala, 2021). Bateman (2022) also argues for increased attention to be paid to empirical studies so as to validate the frameworks presently used in multimodal discourse analysis. In addition to strengthening the analytical approaches, the interpretation of meanings should also be made in view of intersubjective agreement (Husserl, 1907/1964). Following Hasan (1992), the intersubjective position can serve as a shared agreement of the interpretation made of a discourse within a community so as to sift out extreme or incongruous interpretations.

Related to the possible subjectivity of the interpretation is another common criticism of multimodal discourse analysis as neglecting to seek the intentions of the sign maker and elicit feedback from the audience of the discourse (Chen, 2022; Holsanova, 2012). In a study of multimodal classroom discourse analysis, this could involve interviewing the teachers to understand why they have made certain semiotic selections and interviewing the students to understand how they would interpret their teachers' certain semiotic choices. While complementing the multimodal classroom discourse analysis with mixed empirical methods, which include interviews, reflections and focus group discussions, can enrich our understanding of the data and inform the interpretation of our analysis (Bateman et al., 2017), it is just as valid to recognise that adding these methods of reception studies is not compulsory. In the SFMDA approach, we recognise that acts of meaning-making are never arbitrary but motivated by interest (Kress, 1993). However, these choices may not always be conscious or intentional to the sign maker. As such, interviewing the sign maker may not always result in a lucid explanation of why certain semiotic choices have been made as she may hold tacit beliefs and possess values that she may not be fully aware of. The SFMDA approach, as a discourse analysis approach, analyses discourse as an artefact of culture (Gee, 2004) and resists the intentional fallacy in reading. In this, the SFMDA approach shares the view made famous by classical semiotician, Roland Barthes, that 'the birth of the reader must be at the cost of the death of the author' (Barthes, 1977, p. 148).

2.4 Conclusion

The SFMDA approach to understand multimodal classroom discourse can offer researchers a way to make sense of the rich video data collected from lesson observations. It also reveals the nuances in meanings that are made beyond the use of language. In adopting an analytical approach that is multimodal rather than 'linguistic-plus', researchers can attend to the contributions made by each individual semiotic resource as well as the interplay of meanings in their multimodal orchestration. Such an analytical approach can offer researchers and teacher practitioners a deeper understanding of the teacher's embodied teaching and how it can express specific pedagogies. While there are challenges inherent in the SFMDA approach, they are not insurmountable—some can be mediated with careful design and the self-reflexive awareness of the limitations and others can be addressed in time with advancement in digital technologies. Multimodal classroom discourse analysis not just brings implications for education research to understand the nature of teaching and learning in classrooms across contexts but also informs the professional learning of teachers by offering them a lens to reflect on their use of embodied semiotic resources during a lesson to design for purposeful learning experiences for the students.

References

Amundrud, T. (2018). Applying multimodal research to the tertiary foreign language classroom: Looking at gaze. In H. D. S. Joyce & S. Feez (Eds.), *Multimodality across classrooms: Learning about and through different modalities* (pp. 160–177). London and New York: Routledge.

Baldry, A. P., & Thibault, P. (2006). *Multimodal transcription and text analysis.* Equinox Publishing.

Barthes, R. (1977). *Elements of semiology.* Hill and Wang.

Bateman, J. A. (2022). Multimodality, where next?—Some meta-methodological considerations. *Multimodality & Society, 2*(1), 41–63. http://doi.org/10.1177/26349795211073043

Bateman, J. A., Wildfeuer, J., & Hiippala, T. (2017). *Multimodality: Foundations, research and analysis—A problem-oriented introduction.* De Gruyter Mouton.

Bateman, J. (2014). *Text and image: A critical introduction to the visual/verbal divide.* Routledge.

Bateman, J. A., & Hiippala, T. (2021). From data to patterns: on the role of models in empirical multimodality research. In J. Pflaeging, J. Wildfeuer, & J. A. Bateman (Eds.), *Empirical multimodality research: Methods, applications, implications.* De Gruyter.

Bellack, A. A., Kliebard, H. M., Hyman, R. T., & Smith, F. L. (1966). *The language of the classroom.* Teachers College.

Bernstein, B. (1990). *Class, codes and control: Volume IV. The structuring of pedagogic discourse.* Routledge.

Bezemer, J., & Mavers, D. (2011). Multimodal transcription as academic practice: A social semiotic perspective. *International Journal of Social Research Methodology, 13*(3), 191–206. https://doi.org/10.1080/13645579.2011.563616

Boistrup, B. L., & Selander, S. (Eds.). (2022). *Designs for research, teaching and learning. A framework for future education.* Routledge. Open access.

Chen, Y. (2022). Salient visual foci on human faces in viewers' engagement with advertisements: Eye-tracking evidence and theoretical implications. *Multimodality & Society, 2*(1), 3–22. http://doi.org/10.1177/26349795221076361

Christie, F. (1993). Curriculum genres: Planning for effective teaching. In B. Cope & M. Kalantzis (Eds.), *The power of literacy* (pp. 154–178). Routledge.

Christie, F. (2002). *Classroom discourse analysis: A functional perspective.* Continuum.

Cope, B., & Kalantzis, M. (2020). *Making sense—reference, agency, and structure in a grammar of multimodal meaning.* Cambridge University Press.

Diamantopoulou, S., & Orevik, S. (2021). *Multimodality in English language learning.* Routledge.

Edwards, D., & Westgate, D. (1994). *Investigating classroom talk.* The Falmer Press.

Flewitt, R. (2006). Using video to investigate preschool classroom interaction: Education research assumptions and methodological practices. *Visual Communication, 5,* 25–50. https://doi.org/10.1177/1470357206060917

Gee, J. P. (2004). *Situated language and learning: A critique of traditional schooling.* Routledge.

Goodwin, C. (1979). The interactive construction of a sentence in natural conversation. In G. Psathas (Ed.), *Everyday language: Studies in ethnomethodology* (pp. 7–121) New York: Irvington Publishers.

Hall, E. (1966). *The hidden dimension.* Doubleday.

Halliday, M. A. K. (1994). *An introduction to functional grammar* (2nd ed.). Arnold (1st ed., 1985).

Halliday, M. A. K. (1975). *Learning to mean—explorations in the development of language.* Edward Arnold.

Halliday, M. A. K. (1978). *Language as social semiotic: The social interpretation of language and meaning.* Edward Arnold.

Hasan, R. (1992/2009). Rationality in everyday talk: From process to system. In J. J. Webster (Ed.), *Semantic variation: Meaning in society and in sociolinguistics. Collected papers of Ruqaiya Hasan* (Vol. 2, pp. 309–352). Equinox.

Hiippala, T. (2021). Distant viewing and multimodality theory: Prospects and challenges. *Multimodality & Society, 1*(2), 134–152.

Holsanova, J. (2012). New methods for studying visual communication and multimodal integration. *Visual Communication, 11*(3), 251–257.

Hood, S. E. (2007). Gesture and meaning making in face-to-face teaching. *Paper presented at the semiotic margins conference*, University of Sydney.

Hood, S. E. (2011). Body language in face-to-face teaching: A focus on textual and interpersonal meaning. In E. A. Thompson, M. Stenglin, & S. Dreyfus (Eds.), *Semiotic margins: Meaning in multimodalities* (pp. 31–52). Continuum.

Husserl, E. G. A. (1964). *The idea of phenomenology* (W. P. Alston & G. Nakhnikian, Trans.). Nijhoff (Original work published 1907).

Iedema, R. (2001). Analysing film and television a social semiotic account of Hospital an unhealthy business. In T. Van Leeuwen & C. Jewitt (Eds.), *The handbook of visual analysis* (pp. 183–204). Sage.

Jewitt, C., Adami, E., Archer, A., Bjorkvall, A., & Lim, F. V. (2021). Editorial. *Multimodality & Society, 1*(1), 3–7.

Jewitt, C. (2008). *Technology, literacy, learning: A multimodality approach*. Routledge.

Jewitt, C. (Ed.). (2009). *The Routledge handbook of multimodal analysis*. Routledge.

Jewitt, C., Bezemer, J., & O'Halloran, K. L. (2016). *Introducing multimodality*. Routledge.

Knoblauch, H., Schnettler, B., Raab, J., & Soeffner, H.-G. (Eds.). (2009). *Video analysis: Methodology and methods; qualitative audiovisual data analysis in sociology* (2nd ed.). Peter Lang.

Kress, G., & van Leeuwen, T. (2006[1996]). *Reading images: The grammar of visual design*. Routledge.

Kress, G., et al. (2005). *English in urban classrooms: A multimodal perspective on teaching and learning*. Routledge Falmer.

Kress, G., Selander, S., Säljö, R., & Wulf, C. (Eds.). (2021). *Learning as social practice. Beyond education as an individual enterprise*. Routledge.

Kress, G. (1993). Against arbitrariness: The social production of the sign as a foundational issue in critical discourse analysis. Vol. 4, No. 2, SPECIAL ISSUE: Critical Discourse Analysis (1993), pp. 169–19. *Discourse & Society.* https://doi.org/10.1177/0957926593004002003

Kress, G. (2010). *Multimodality—A social semiotic approach to contemporary communication*. Routledge.

Kuckartz, U., & Radiker, S. (2019). *Analyzing qualitative data with MAXQDA: Text, audio, and video*. Springer.

Lemke, J. (1995). *Textual politics: Discourse and social dynamics*. Taylor & Francis.

Lim, F. V., & O'Halloran, K. L. (2012). The ideal teacher: Analysis of a teacher-recruitment advertisement. *Semiotica, 189*, 229–253.

Lim, F. V., O'Halloran, K. L., & Podlasov, A. (2012). Spatial pedagogy: Mapping meanings in the use of classroom space. *Cambridge Journal of Education, 42*(2), 235–251.

Lim, F. V. (2011). *A systemic functional multimodal discourse analysis approach to pedagogic discourse* (PhD dissertation, National University of Singapore).

Lim, F. V. (2019). Analysing the teachers' use of gestures in the classroom: A systemic functional multimodal discourse analysis. *Social Semiotics, 29*(1), 83–111.

Lim, F. V. (2021a). *Designing learning with embodied teaching: Perspectives from multimodality*. Routledge. London, New York.

Lim, F. V. (2021b). Investigating intersemiosis: A systemic functional multimodal discourse analysis of the relationship between language and gesture in classroom discourse. *Visual Communication, 20*(1), 34–58.

Liu, Y., & O'Halloran, K. L. (2009). Intersemiotic texture: Analyzing cohesive devices between language and images. *Social Semiotics, 19*(4), 367–388.

Martinec, R. (2000). Construction of identity in Michael Jackson's "Jam". *Social Semiotics, 10*(3), 313–329. http://doi.org/10.1080/10350330050136370

Martinec, R. (2001). Interpersonal resources in action. *Semiotica, 135*, 117–145. http://doi.org/10.1515/semi.2001.056

Mehan, H. (1979). *Learning lessons: Social organization in the classroom*. Harvard University Press.

Mercer, N. (2000). *Words and minds: How we use language to think together*. Routledge

Mercer, J. (2007). The challenges of insider research in educational institutions: Wielding a double-edged sword and resolving delicate dilemmas. *Oxford Review of Education, 33*(1), 1–17. http://doi.org/10.1080/03054980601094651

Mondada, L. (2016). Challenges of multimodality: Language and the body in social interaction. *Journal of Sociolinguistics, 20*(3), 336–366.

O'Halloran, K. L. (2005). *Mathematical discourse: Language, symbolism and visual images*. Continuum.

O'Halloran, K. L., & Lim, F. V. (2014). Systemic functional multimodal discourse analysis. In S. Norris & C. Maier (Eds.), *Texts, images and interactions: A reader in multimodality* (pp. 135–154). De Gruyter.

O'Halloran, K. L. (2011). Multimodal discourse analysis. In K. Hyland & B. Paltridge (Eds.), *Companion to discourse* (pp. 120–137). Continuum.

O'Halloran, K. L., Pal, G., & Jin, M. (2021). Multimodal approach to analysing big social and news media data. *Discourse, Context & Media, 40*, 100467.

O'Halloran, K. L., Podlasov, A., Chua, A., & Marissa, K. L. E. (2012). Interactive software for multimodal analysis. *Visual Communication, 11*(3), 363–381. https://doi.org/10.1177/1470357212446414

O'Halloran, K. L. (2004). Discourses in secondary school mathematics classrooms according to social class and gender. In J. A. Foley (Ed.), *Language, education and discourse: Functional approaches* (pp. 191–255). Continuum.

O'Toole, M. (2010[1994]). *The language of displayed art*. Routledge.

Ochs, E., Pontecorvo, C., & Fasulo, A. (1996). Socializing taste. *Ethnos, 6*(1), 7–46.

Ochs, E. (1979). Transcription as theory. In E. Ochs & B. B. Schieffelin (Eds.), *Developmental pragmatics* (pp. 43–72). Academic Press.

Royce, T. (1998). Synergy on the page: Exploring intersemiotic complementarity in page-based multimodal text. *JASFL Occasional Articles, 1*, 25–49.

Royce, T. (2006). Intersemiotic complementarity: A framework for multimodal discourse analysis. In T. Royce & W. L. Bowcher (Eds.), *New directions in the analysis of multimodal discourse* (pp. 63–109). Lawrence Erlbaum.

Savery, J. R., & Duffy, T. M. (1995). Problem based learning: An instructional model and its constructivist framework. In B. Wilson (Ed.), *Constructivist learning environments: Case studies in instructional design* (pp. 135–150). Technology Publications.

Seedhouse, P. (2004). Conversation analysis methodology. *Language Learning, a Journal of Research in Language Studies*, *54*(1), 1–54. https://doi.org/10.1111/j.1467-9922.2004.00268.x

Schegloff, E. A. (1984). On some gestures' relation to talk. In A. Maxwell & J. Heritage (Eds.), *Structures of social action* (pp. 266–296). Cambridge University Press.

Sinclair, J., & Coulthard, M. (1975). *Towards an analysis of discourse: The English used by teachers and pupils*. Oxford University Press.

Stenglin, M. K. (2009). Space odyssey: Towards a social semiotic model of three-dimensional space. *Visual Communication*, 8(1), 35–64. https://doi.org/10.1177/1470357208099147

Takahashi, J., & Yu, D. (2017). Multimodality in the classroom: An introduction. *Working Articles in TESOL & Applied Linguistics*, *16*(2), i–vi.

Vygotsky, L. S. (1978). *Mind in society: The development of higher psychological processes*. Harvard University Press.

Walsh, S. (2006). *Investigating classroom discourse*. Routledge.

Weninger, C., Lim, F. V., & Chen, Y. (forthcoming). Applying multimodal analysis. In R. Mehdi (Ed.), *Less frequently used methodologies and procedures in applied linguistics*. John Benjamins.

Wittenburg, P., Brugman, H., Russel, A., Klassmann, A., & Sloetjes, H. (2006). ELAN: A professional framework for multimodality research [paper presentation]. *The international conference on language resources and evaluation*, Genoa, Italy.

3 The use of epistemic network analysis in analysing classroom discourse in EMI-science classrooms

Kason Ka Ching Cheung and Jack K. H. Pun

3.1 Project overview and context

Many countries in Europe promoted the notion of Content and Language Integrated Learning (CLIL) (Pérez-Cañado, 2012). The principle behind CLIL is that students can integrate language and content learning within an authentic context (Lo & Lin, 2015). As they (2015) argued, CLIL has a view which classroom teaching should break the boundary of teaching canonical content *only*. Canonical content can be used as a tool to extend students' L2 learning experience. We argue the importance of CLIL owing to the following two reasons: (1) CLIL has been a theoretical perspective to explore classroom discourse in Hong Kong science classroom (Lin & Wu, 2014; Lo, 2014); (2) content and language should be both prioritised in science classrooms (Pun & Cheung, 2021).

In Hong Kong, there is a strong parental demand for students to access English-medium schools (Lin, 2012). Hong Kong secondary schools are classified into English-medium instruction (EMI) secondary schools and Chinese-medium instruction (CMI) secondary schools (Lin & Man, 2009) before 2010. However, after September 2010, CMI secondary schools are permitted to use English as a medium of instruction in some of the non-language subjects (Lin & Man, 2009). For example, the school where the second author is working is originally a CMI school. Some of the biology classes are taught in English, whereas some of the biology classes are taught in Chinese. The CMI secondary schools have the autonomy to enforce policies on the medium of instruction (MOI) on non-language subjects. When they enforce the MOI policy, there is a major challenge: students do not possess the English language ability to learn science in lessons with only L2 instruction (Lin, 2012).

Our project aims to investigate how teachers and students draw on and *link* different semiotic resources in CLIL-based science classrooms. However, there is only a scarcity of research studies, which use a qualitative method that characterises the *link* of semiotic resources in CLIL-based science classrooms. These resources are L1, L2 and multimodal resources (Evnitskaya & Morton, 2011; Li, 2015). To understand the abstract science concepts, the use of L1 reduces the barriers to learning science of L2 (Lo, 2014). Common research methodologies in this area of research are dialogue coding (Pun & Macaro, 2018), lengths of teachers' and students' turns using L1 and L2 (Lo, 2014) or multimodal conversational analysis (Tai & Wei, 2020). Researchers in this field pay particular attention to the frequency and the type of codes (i.e. L1 and L2) in each turn of the talk. Research studies in the future should use a method that combines the frequency and the type of codes together in studying complex classroom dynamics in EMI-science classrooms.

In this chapter, we illustrate the use of a method, *Epistemic Network Analysis* (ENA) (Shaffer et al., 2016), which captures the frequency and the type of codes in studying the use of semiotic resources in CLIL-based science classrooms. An ENA is originally modelling cognitive networks, but it has been applied to discourse analysis in curriculum and assessment (Cheung, 2020), different students' integration of multimodal resources (Cheung & Winterbottom, 2021) and interactions in learning space (Vujovic et al., 2021). Its use in analysing discourse in CLIL-based science classrooms is novel. ENA will visualise how frequent the connections of codes are in networks, so it allows qualitative comparison of networks between individual students, between students and teachers, as well as between teachers of a variety of backgrounds and experiences.

3.2 Research planning and design

We choose the 'rainbow diagram' from Lin (2012) as our project conceptual framework because of two reasons: (1) CLIL requires teachers to draw on multiple semiotic resources to scaffold students to integrate content and language learning, including valuing L1 and (2) her framework emphasises on the *links* between L1 and L2 every day, oral and written language, as well as visuals and multimodalities. The *links* enable us to develop a coding scheme and use ENA to visualise these links between codes. If there is not any link among categories, ENA might not be useful in creating networks among categories. Therefore, careful attention should be paid to choosing a theoretical framework or conceptual framework in studying EMI classrooms.

Based on this framework, we aim at studying how teachers and students link these semiotic resources in science classrooms. More interestingly, we can compare how teachers and students link these semiotic resources in different contexts, for example, in the context of practical work (Pun & Cheung, 2021), discussing scientific representations (Cheung & Winterbottom, 2021a, 2021b) or argumentation.

3.3 Research context

To answer the research questions above, this study carries out a qualitative discourse analysis to identify the moments during a practical work session (Pun & Cheung, 2021; Pun & Tai, 2021). We have examined an archive of videos from a project which studied classroom interactions in senior-form EMI science classrooms in Hong Kong. In particular, we are interested in analysing how teachers and students draw on different semiotic resources of make meaning of practical work. Practical work is a context in which teachers and students are required to draw on multiple semiotic resources, for example, didactic gestures, apparatuses and textbook diagrams (Pun & Cheung, 2021). Therefore, we select one lesson episode from an EMI school where students and teachers construct knowledge behind a practical work activity. In this lesson, students were measuring the electroconductivity of different acids and alkalis in order to find out the strength of acids and alkalis. The teacher introduced the scientific concepts behind the practical work by explaining how the strengths of acids and alkalis can be related to the degree of dissociation of ions. They did not learn how to measure the electroconductivity and the teacher allowed them to explore the practical set-up. However, they had some prior knowledge which includes the understandings of current and power when they had science lessons in Year 8. The teacher has a degree in chemistry and a teacher training certificate. He has 5–6 years of teaching experience.

3.4 ENA

ENA creates networks based on weighted structured connections (Shaffer & Ruis, 2017). In discourse analysis, we often see that two codes are related to each other in a single turn. The method will create networks based on the weighted frequency of connections between two codes in a single *stanza*. The idea of the stanza is that (1) codes within a stanza are related to each other and (2) codes in different stanzas are not related to each other (Shaffer & Ruis, 2017). In the following paragraphs, we are going to illustrate how this method can be applied to studying how teachers and students draw on different semiotic resources in EMI science classrooms.

The first step of ENA is to come up with codes to analyse classroom interactions. These codes should be informed by a sound conceptual framework. The lesson was video-recorded and transcribed bilingually and multimodally. A follow-up interview was carried out with the teacher on his perception of using EMI in teaching science. We read the transcript and carry out discourse analysis. Researchers claimed that discourse analysis should be inductive in nature, as they believed that the reality is fluid and socially constructed (Hardy et al., 2004). However, due to the nature of ENA, the codes should be uniform across the transcript so that there can comparison between teachers' and students' use of multilingual and multimodal resources. Therefore, we should have a preliminary conceptual framework in our mind (Bressler et al., 2019), that is Lin (2012)'s rainbow diagram. The first level of codes based on the framework are L1 academic written language, L1 academic oral language, L1 everyday oral language, L2 academic written language, L2 academic oral language and L2 everyday oral language. For the multimodal representations, we code the transcript using the codes by Pun and Cheung (2021). These include gestures, texts, diagrams and objects.

The second step is to examine whether the codes in the conceptual framework can be applied to the lesson transcript. In fact, for discourse analysis, we should not assume that all codes can be applied to the transcript. There is always something interesting arisen from the data. As a research team, we examined the transcript of the lesson episode together. We came into a consensus that it was not necessary to differentiate between oral and written language because we studied the oral interaction between students and teachers. Therefore, regarding the codes on dialogue, we generated four codes: L1 non-academic language, L1 academic language, L2 non-academic language and L2 academic language. Moreover, for multimodal representations, we inductively generated some codes after examining the transcript: gestures (pointing), gestures (representation), texts, diagrams and objects. Gestures or gesticulations refer to the movement of arms and body which accompany talking (Williams, 2020). In the lesson episode, we identified two types of gestures, pointing gestures (deictic) (Williams, 2020) and representational gestures. Pointing refers to using fingers or hands to locate a particular object or event; representational gestures refer to how students use body movement to demonstrate a scientific concept. Table 3.1 shows the name of the categories, short forms of the categories shown in epistemic networks and examples in our transcript.

The next step is to define the stanza and plan what we aim to compare. As a simple illustration, we define one *stanza* as one turn. Codes in one turn are related to each other, while codes in different turns are not related to each other. Our aims are to compare how different teachers and students draw on multilingual and multimodal resources. Moreover, we aim to compare teachers' and students' use of multimodal and multilingual resources in three different types of settings: (1) when the teacher was lecturing and questioning students; (2) when students were carrying out their own practical work activities *without* the teacher's supervision; and (3) when the students were carrying out practical work activities *with* the teacher's supervision. Therefore, we labelled each turn with the type of person speaking, as well as segmenting the transcript into three different types of episodes.

We then input our coding into an excel file. In the excel file, we entered '1' into the present code and entered '0' for the absent code (see examples from Figure 3.1). After checking the entry of our data, we input the excel file into www.epistemicnetwork.org/.

Table 3.1 Categories for coding the lesson transcript

Categories	Codes	Short form of the codes	Examples
Language resources	L1 academic language	L1 Non-Acad Lang	咦你地做到啦咁勁既 (You guys are so powerful).
	L1 non-academic oral language	L1 Acad Vocab	氯氣囉 (chlorine)
	L2 academic language	L2 Non-Acad Lang	**Today we are going to do an experiment** to compare the strength of acids. I didn't use the lab manual. And I hope you ready. We are going to compare the strength of acid and alkali.
	L2 Non-academic language	L2 Acad Vocab	唔好開咁大，有**chlorine gas**。(Don't turn to high power as there will be chlorine gas produced.)
Multimodal resources	Gestures (pointing)	Gest.P	(The student is pointing at the multimeter.)
	Gestures (representation)	Gest.R	(The teacher uses gesture to show the curve of alternative current.)
	Texts	Text	(The student is referring to the text.)
	Diagrams	Diagram	(The teacher is pointing the diagram in the manual.)
	Objects	Object	(manipulating the object)

Turn	Episode	Person	Type of P	Transcript	L1 Non-Acad Lang	L1 Acad Vocab	L2 Non-Acad Lang	L2 Acad Vocab	Gest.P	Gest.R	Text	Diagram	Object
1	Lecture	T	T	Today we are going to do an experiment to compare the strength of acids. I didn't use the lab manual. And I hope you ready. We are going to compare the strength of acid and alkali. First Part A. we use this experiment to this set up to test for the conductivity of acid. Conductivity, the second test is pH. Acid we have test. First test is acid, second test is pH. For alkali it will be the same. I think most of you have trouble to connect the electrical circuit. Try to connect it by yourself first. If you have any difficulties, if you have any problems. I am going to help you. I hope you can connect by yourself. In my experience, all students have bad results. Last but not least ammeter, is it series or parallel? Ammeter? Connect in series or parallel? (wait) What is ammeter? Ammeter is used to connect current. Connect in series or parallel?	0	0	1	1	0	0	0	1	0
2	Lecture	S	S	Series	0	0	0	1	0	0	0	0	0
3	Lecture	T	T	Series please.	0	0	0	1	0	0	0	0	0
4	Lecture	T	T	Ammeter. And then the electrode. And then this is the solution. And then the power. Ok pay attention. The multimeter, that means the ammeter will be over there. On your right hand side.	0	0	1	1	0	0	0	0	0
5	Lecture		T	The power supply. Pay attention. The power supply will be here. Try to connect it by yourself. The solutions is over there. Ethanoic acid, sulphuric acid and ammonium solution are over there. Please take what you need for your bench and start doing it by yourself. Go!	0	0	1	1	0	0	0	0	0
6	Gp work_5	S1	S	錶個D solution	1	0	0	1	0	0	0	0	0
7	Gp work_5	S2	S	50 cm cube of 一mole ethanoic acid into small beaker. 80 cm cube 呀	1	0	0	1	0	0	1	0	0
8	Gp work_5	S3	S	Connect the wire.	0	0	1	0	0	0	0	0	1
9	Gp work_5	S2	S	Connect the wire	0	0	1	0	0	0	0	0	0
10	Gp work_5	S4	S	呀sir 係咪用呢D來裝	1	0	0	0	0	0	0	0	0

Figure 3.1 Input of codes into the excel file

Epistemic network analysis in EMI discourse 39

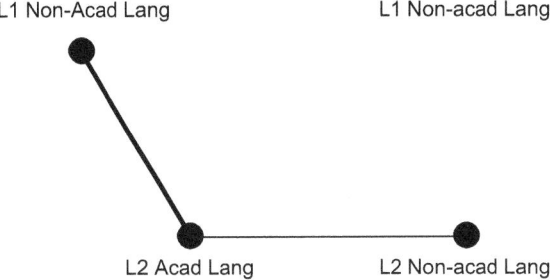

Figure 3.2 Hypothetical example of a network generated

Epistemic networks will be generated after entering the excel file into the programme. Figure 3.2 shows a hypothetical example of a network generated in a science lesson episode. A thicker line joining two codes indicates that these two codes appear in one turn at a higher frequency, while a thinner line joining two codes indicates that these two codes appear in one turn at a lower frequency. In Figure 3.2, the line joining 'L1 Non-Acad Lang' and 'L2 Acad Lang' is the thickest. This shows that in this particular episode, both L1 non-academic language and L2 academic language are simultaneously drawn in a lot of turns. Comparatively speaking, the line joining 'L2 Acad Lang' and 'L2 Non-acad Lang' is less thick. Therefore, we can draw a conclusion that the simultaneous use of L2 non-academic language and L2 academic language is less than that of L1 non-academic language and L2 academic language. However, there is not any connection between 'L1 Non-acad Lang' and 'L2 Non-acad Lang', so L1 non-academic language and L2 non-academic language do not simultaneously appear in any turn.

3.5 Strengths of ENA in analysing classroom interactions

In CLIL classrooms, we should not consider language or multimodal representations as individual, separate resources (Lin, 2012). Students and teachers use these semiotic resources simultaneously in science CLIL-based classrooms. Therefore, we need an innovative method to visualise the connections between these resources, ENA in CLIL-based science classrooms.

One major advantage of this method is that it allows comparison of how different people draw on different semiotic resources in CLIL-based science classrooms. Figure 3.3 shows an example of how the teacher and the students draw on different resources. From the results, there is a thick line joining 'L1. Non. Acad. Lang' and 'L2.Acad.Vocab', showing that L1 non-academic language and L2 academic language are intertwined in science EMI classrooms.

The use of 'L1.Acad.Vocab' (L1 academic language) is not frequently linked to the classroom interaction in the practical work setting. Different modes of representations, such as gesture (pointing), gesture (representing) and objects, are connected to the language resources.

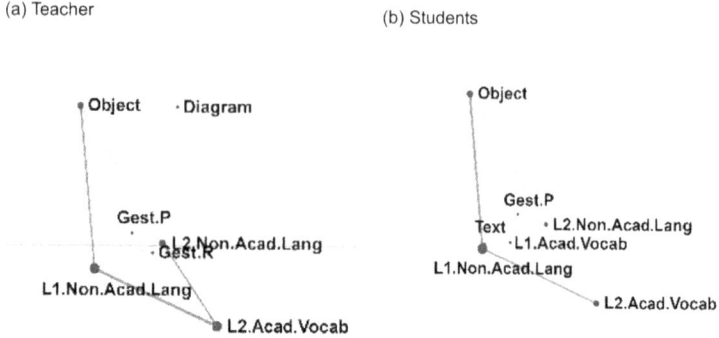

Figure 3.3 Epistemic networks of (a) the teacher and (b) students (only connected codes shown)

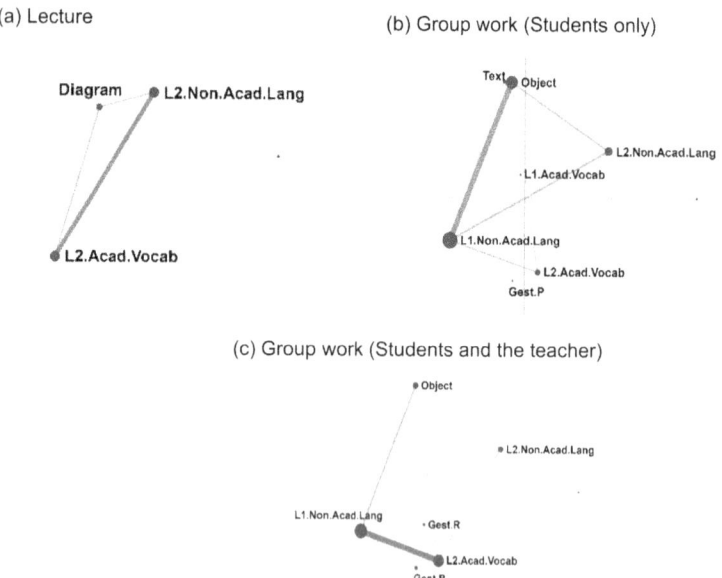

Figure 3.4 Epistemic networks of teachers and students during (a) lecture; (b) group work (students only); and (c) group with (with the supervision of teachers)

Another advantage of this method is that it aids comparison of different episodes when students and teachers draw on different semiotic resources in CLIL-based science classrooms. When we compare networks in Figure 3.4, we can see the use of L1 academic language and L1 non-academic language begins to evolve in the group work setting instead of in the lecture part. More importantly, when we compare Figure 3.4(b) and Figure 3.4(c), the presence of both L1 non-academic language (L1.Non.Acad.Lang) and L2 academic language (L2.Lang.Vocab) in one turn was more frequent when the teacher was accompanying the students. This might show that the teacher helped students use L1 non-academic language to build up their knowledge of L2 academic language.

3.6 Overcoming the weaknesses in ENA in analysing classroom interactions

Though this method is effective in comparing discourse between objects or different episodes, it has two disadvantages: (1) readers do not understand the socio-cultural context by understanding interpreting the network and (2) although the connections between codes were shown in the networks, we do not understand what type of connections. Therefore, it is necessary for EMI researchers to describe the context of the lesson episode which couple ENA. It will be also beneficial if EMI researchers can illustrate some examples of multimodal transcript to show, for example, how representational gesturing supports the construction of L2 academic language. Table 3.2 shows an episode when the student was learning the difference between direct current and alternating current from the teacher. There was a switch in the multimeter which allowed the students to choose between direct current and alternating current. The students were confused by the choice between the direct current and the alternating current. The teacher understood that using only L2 might not be able to help students understand the science concept. Therefore, he used L1 non-academic language '會轉既' (the current will change) and '有個波浪' (it takes the shape of wave) to scaffold students' learning of L2 academic vocabularies. He also used his figures to gesture the shape of the wave and show the differences between direct current and alternating current.

A showcase of exemplary transcript and a thick description of the context will help readers to understand the connections between gesture (representation), L1 non-academic language as well as L2 academic language. As indicated by the thin line among the three codes ('Gest.R', 'L1.Non.Acad.Lang' and 'L2.Acad.Vocab'), we can see the synergistic effects of L1 non-academic language and representational gesturing support non-native English speakers in learning science in an EMI-science classroom. This will enrich the description of how teachers and students draw on different semiotic resources in CLIL-based science classrooms.

Table 3.2 Example of multimodal representations support language learning

Persons	Transcript	Multimodal representations
S2	Direct current?	
T	有架。我知啦你無按到呢度。 (Yes, you should press here (direct current)).	
S2	咩意思呀? (What's the meaning?)	
T	呢個係AC 呢個係DC (This is AC. This is DC) 呢個係AC alternating current,即係會轉既,有個波浪 (This one is AC, alternating current. It will change its current. It takes a shape of waves.) 呢個DC係直線 (DC is a straight line)	Gesturing alternative current

3.7 Conclusion

ENA is a useful method to visualise how teachers and students draw on different semiotic resources in CLIL-based science classrooms. We have explored how teachers and students draw on the following semiotic resources in the context of science practical work: L1 academic language, L1 non-academic language, L2 academic language, L2 non-academic language, gestures (representation), gestures (pointing), texts, objects and diagrams. In this chapter, we have created five epistemic networks. These networks show how these elements of resources are linked together by teachers and students respectively in three different contexts, namely lecturing, group work without teacher's supervision and group work under teacher's supervision.

This method can be used to compare the differences between teachers and students in drawing semiotic resources in the same turn, as well as how teachers and students mobilise these resources simultaneously in different lesson contexts. This method breaks the boundary of coding turns and counts the frequency of codes which appear. We notice that research studies in EMI classrooms attempt to make comparison between native and non-native teachers (Inbar-Lourie & Donitsa-Schmidt, 2019), as well as before and after professional development workshops with teachers. This method offers researchers a valuable tool for comparison.

However, this method has two limitations: (1) readers do not understand the socio-cultural context by understanding interpreting the network and (2) although the connections between codes were shown in the networks, we do not understand what type of connections. These limitations can be counterbalanced by having a thick description of the context and showing an example of the lesson transcript. This will enrich the discussion of the findings arisen from ENA.

Funding

This work was funded in part by the National Science Foundation (DRL-1661036, DRL-1713110), the Wisconsin Alumni Research Foundation and the Office of the Vice Chancellor for Research and Graduate Education at the University of Wisconsin-Madison. The opinions, findings and conclusions do not reflect the views of the funding agencies, cooperating institutions or other individuals.

References

Bressler, D. M., Bodzin, A. M., Eagan, B., & Tabatabai, S. (2019). Using epistemic network analysis to examine discourse and scientific practice during a collaborative game. *Journal of Science Education and Technology, 28*(5), 553–566.

Cheung, K. K. C. (2020). Exploring the inclusion of nature of science in biology curriculum and high-stakes assessments in Hong Kong. *Science & Education, 29*(3), 491–512.

Cheung, K. K. C., & Winterbottom, M. (2021a). Exploring students' visualisation competence with photomicrographs of villi. *International Journal of Science Education, 43*(14), 2290–2315.

Cheung, K. K. C., & Winterbottom, M. (2021b). Students' integration of textbook representations into their understanding of photomicrographs: epistemic network analysis. *Research in Science & Technological Education*, 1–20.

Evnitskaya, N., & Morton, T. (2011). Knowledge construction, meaning-making and interaction in CLIL science classroom communities of practice. *Language and Education, 25*(2), 109–127.

Hardy, C., Harley, B., & Phillips, N. (2004). Discourse analysis and content analysis: Two solitudes. *Qualitative Methods, 2*, 19–22. http://doi.org/10.5281/zenodo.998649

Inbar-Lourie, O., & Donitsa-Schmidt, S. (2019). EMI lecturers in international universities: Is a native/non-native English-speaking background relevant? *International Journal of Bilingual Education and Bilingualism, 23*(3), 301–313.

Li, D. C. S. (2015). Discussion: L1 as semiotic resource in content cum L2 learning at secondary level—empirical evidence from Hong Kong. *International Journal of Bilingual Education and Bilingualism, 18*(3), 336–344.

Lin, A. M. Y. (2012). 5. multilingual and multimodal resources in genre-based pedagogical approaches to L2 English content classrooms. In *English—A changing medium for education* (pp. 79–103) Multilingual Matters.

Lin, A. M. Y., & Man, E. Y. (2009). *Bilingual education: Southeast Asian perspectives.* Hong Kong University Press.

Lin, A. M. Y., & Wu, Y. (2014). "May I speak cantonese?"—Co-constructing a scientific proof in an EFL junior secondary science classroom. *International Journal of Bilingual Education and Bilingualism, 18*(3), 289–305.

Lo, Y. Y. (2014). How much L1 is too much? Teachers' language use in response to students' abilities and classroom interaction in content and language integrated learning. *International Journal of Bilingual Education and Bilingualism, 18*(3), 270–288.

Lo, Y. Y., & Lin, A. M. Y. (2015). Special issue: Designing multilingual and multimodal CLIL frameworks for EFL students. *International Journal of Bilingual Education and Bilingualism, 18*(3), 261–269.

Pérez-Cañado, M. L. (2012). CLIL research in Europe: Past, present, and future. *International Journal of Bilingual Education and Bilingualism, 15*(3), 315–341.

Pun, J. K. H., & Cheung, K. K. C. (2021). Meaning making in collaborative practical work: A case study of multimodal challenges in a Year 10 chemistry classroom. *Research in Science & Technological Education*, 1–18.

Pun, J. K. H., & Macaro, E. (2018). The effect of first and second language use on question types in English medium instruction science classrooms in Hong Kong. *International Journal of Bilingual Education and Bilingualism, 22*(1), 64–77.

Pun, J. K. H., & Tai, K. W. H. (2021). Doing science through translanguaging: A study of translanguaging practices in secondary English as a medium of instruction science laboratory sessions. *International Journal of Science Education, 43*(7), 1112–1139.

Shaffer, D. W., Collier, W., & Ruis, A. R. (2016). A tutorial on epistemic network analysis: Analyzing the structure of connections in cognitive, social, and interaction data. *Journal of Learning Analytics, 3*(3), 9–45.

Shaffer, D. W., & Ruis, A. R. (2017). Epistemic network analysis: A worked example of theory-based learning analytics. In *Handbook of learning analytics* (pp. 175–187). Scholar Society for Learning Analytics Research.

Tai, K. W. H., & Wei, L. (2020). Co-learning in Hong Kong English medium instruction mathematics secondary classrooms: A translanguaging perspective. *Language and Education, 35*(3), 241–267.

Vujovic, M., Amarasinghe, I., & Hernandez-Leo, D. (2021). Studying collaboration dynamics in physical learning spaces: Considering the temporal perspective through epistemic network analysis. *Sensors (Basel), 21*(9). www.ncbi.nlm.nih.gov/pubmed/33919062

Williams, M. (2020). Fifth graders' use of gesture and models when translanguaging during a content and language integrated science class in Hong Kong. *International Journal of Bilingual Education and Bilingualism*, 1–20.

4 Using corpus linguistics and grounded theory to explore EMI stakeholders' discourse

Niall Curry and Pascual Pérez-Paredes

4.1 Introduction

Typically, thematic analyses of interview data employ common-sense approaches where researchers first transcribe interviews, then read the transcripts, highlight emerging themes, and refine these emerging themes throughout the reading process (King et al., 2018). Such an approach necessitates that the researcher identifies distinctive themes, observes some degree of repetition of themes and can use the findings to speak about the group of participants as a whole, using thematic coding approaches, such as grounded theory (Hadley, 2017). As the process involves multiple stages of description, interpretation and synthesis, and requires that analyses consider themes within and across a number of texts, there is a value in investigating the affordances of corpus linguistics approaches to interview analysis, given that corpus linguistics shares these considerations.

To this end, this chapter shows how a corpus linguistics methodology can offer a nuanced approach to thematic coding when used in synchrony with the analytical and conceptual frameworks: grounded theory (Hadley, 2017) and, in the case of English-medium instruction (EMI), the ROAD-MAPPING framework (Dafouz & Smit, 2020). The chapter argues that the use of keyword analysis to generate initial open field codes as part of a grounded theory approach to thematic analysis serves to reveal specific points in interviews and focus groups in which important themes are socially and discursively constructed. Building on previously undertaken studies of interviews and focus groups with EMI lecturers (e.g., Curry & Pérez-Paredes, 2021; Pérez-Paredes & Curry, 2022), the chapter presents a brief, illustrative analysis of the discursive construction of the Roles of English (Dafouz & Smit, 2020) to demonstrate the reflexivity and value of a corpus linguistics informed approach as a way to make sense of complex qualitative data. In so doing, it informs the use of existing analytical and theoretical approaches to studying EMI, presenting, in detail, a methodological approach that can be used to navigate existing EMI interpretative frameworks or taxonomies. To illustrate the proposed method, the analysis is applied to five interviews and two focus groups with English-medium education in a multilingual university setting (EMEMUS) lecturers from a Spanish university.

In what follows, Section 4.2 sets a foundation through a literature review that considers the current state-of-the-art in EMI interview and focus group analysis. Subsequently, Section 4.3 presents a method of combining corpus methodologies with analytical and theoretical frameworks to support a top-down and bottom-up conceptual framework. Next, Section 4.4 presents a short case study, demonstrating the application of the approach outlined in Section 4.3 to interview and focus group data. The chapter concludes in Section 4.5 by offering guidance to EMI researchers on using this method going forward and further directions for methodological innovation.

4.2 Literature review

This section presents an overview of the current state of the art in methodological approaches to analysing interviews and focus groups in EMI research, drawing first on top-down and bottom-up approaches, in Section 4.2.1, and second, on corpus linguistics and grounded theory for analysing interviews and focus groups, in Section 4.2.2.

4.2.1 Analysing interviews and focus groups in EMI research

The value of interviews and focus groups to EMI research is well established in the literature. From a top-down perspective, interviews have been used to demonstrate the affordances of EMI for developing cultural competencies and awareness (Huang & Fang, 2022) and for developing language policy in EMI contexts (Erkan & Dikilitaş, 2022). The role of top-down frameworks being used to understand policy through interview analysis is reflected elsewhere, where, for example, in Pérez-Paredes and Curry (2022), focus groups afford insight into lecturers' perceptions of internationalisation and glocalisation processes in higher education, showing that lecturers play a critical role in translating (or not) internationalisation policy into practice.

These studies are exemplary of top-down approaches, drawing on existing EMI frameworks to code interviews and focus groups, for example Larzen-Ostermark's (2008) theoretical framework is adopted in Huang and Fang (2022), who code interviews in terms of cognitive, action, and affective cultural instruction. Such an approach affords the quintessential advantages of top-down approaches, where the pre-existing notions applied to the data allow researchers to replicate and compare studies. However, there are also limitations in such work. That is because top-down approaches can limit researchers from considering findings in terms beyond a chosen framework and, when working across cultures and spaces, can result in ethnocentric and culturally imposed perspectives. This does not undermine the value and contribution of such work, but it draws attention to the methodological implications of using top-down approaches and the need to consider the affordances of other means to analyse interviews and focus groups, such as bottom-up approaches.

As with top-down approaches, bottom-up approaches to interview and focus group analysis have played a critical role in EMI research. Specifically, bottom-up approaches have been integral to the development of theoretical and conceptual frameworks that respond, in a bespoke manner, to the data being studied. For example, in the focus on the context of EMI in Asia, themes pertaining to languages used in the classroom, perceived benefits, access to specialised knowledge, enhanced employability, intercultural understanding and enhanced mobility emerge as key discursive constructions of EMI in Galloway et al. (2020) and, in Chang (2019), bottom-up approaches are integral to the unpacking of culturally situated EMI policy in the Chinese context through the use of the nexus of practice approach.

The approaches shared by these EMI studies involve a detailed and exploratory means of coding interviews and focus groups, and in these studies, and others like them, the affordances of the bottom-up approaches allow for the identification and evaluation of EMI without the constraints of pre-existing notions framing the analysis. However, bottom-up studies are inherently less comparable and require careful coding to ensure accuracy and consistency. Moreover, the prospect of the perpetual creation of new and distinctive conceptual frameworks means that it will become challenging to gain an overall perspective on the current state of EMI, globally. These critiques of bottom-up approaches do not indicate a strong deficit in this approach. Rather, they highlight the need to be able to reflexively move between top-down and bottom-up approaches.

Following this reasoning, EMI research has benefited from combined top-down and bottom-up approaches. For example, Hu and Lei (2014) describe a multiphased approach to analysing interviews where top-down concepts, following Spolsky's (2009) tripartite language policy framework, are combined with a bottom-up endeavour to reanalyse texts that did not fit neatly within the framework. This is done with a view to identifying new themes beyond those presented by Spolsky (2009). Similarly, Jon et al. (2020) use evaluation coding (Saldaña, 2013) as a means to code EMI-themed interviews with professors in terms of purpose, effectiveness, criticism, and implications but, adopting a bottom-up perspective, remain open to emerging themes. These studies offer valuable examples of the affordances of such a combined approach for maintaining both comparability and cultural sensitivity in EMI research.

As a combined approach, the top-down and bottom-up analysis of interviews and focus groups draws on the affordances of each approach. Arguably, combined top-down and bottom-up approaches are most effective for moving the field of EMI forward, by tweaking, updating, and evolving existing frameworks and allowing for sustained comparison across studies, spanning both time and space. However, challenges remain in the use of combined top-down and bottom-up approaches in and beyond EMI research, owing in part to the time-consuming nature of bottom-up approaches and the bridging of bottom-up emerging frameworks with top-down, pre-existing frameworks (e.g., Dafouz & Smit, 2020; Hu & Lei, 2014). To address the challenge of finding a way into the data that is systematic, objective, expedient, and critical, corpus linguistics and grounded theory can offer recourse.

4.2.2 Affordances of corpus linguistics and grounded theory methodologies

Corpus linguistics, as a research methodology, involves the systematic collection and computational analysis of texts. The approach is founded on core principles of representativeness and sampling whereby the data, known as a corpus or the plural corpora, are designed to represent a subset of language users, defined by their demographic information, textual metadata, and communicative practices. Drawing on corpus analysis software, for example AntConc (Anthony, 2022), or coding programmes, for example R, corpora are typically analysed to identify frequent language use, how that language is used in context, as well as notable collocations, keywords, language patterns, clusters, and lexico-grammatical profiles occurring in the data, for example. While often perceived as a quantitative methodology (O'Halloran, 2014), corpus linguistics has well-established affordances for mixed and qualitative research. Corpus pragmatics (Aijmer & Rühlemann, 2015) and function-to-form studies (Curry, 2022), for example, reflect a keen focus on context and meaning within texts. Such approaches use corpora as a means to access the functional language in texts that performs a critical role in socially constructing discourses.

While the importance of representativeness and sampling is critical to most corpus-based studies, for qualitative studies of interviews and focus groups in EMI research, for example, these principles take on a different dimension to that found in linguistic research (i.e., Sinclair, 2004). Instead, the value of corpus linguistics lies in its capacity to act as a way into the data. In education contexts, Pérez-Paredes (2020) discusses the potential affordances of corpus linguistics for researching educationally relevant textual data, highlighting the value of frequency and keyness for gaining an insight into the content of texts and their social construction against the backdrop of mainstream and diverging language usage in a community of speakers or, for example, professionals.

In a similar vein, Hadley (2017) has discussed in detail the affordances of grounded theory for operationalising corpus linguistics in qualitative research, arguing that there are natural overlaps in the approaches; that is, both corpus linguistics and grounded theory share a focus on real-life data. In his critique of qualitative approaches in corpus linguistics, for example critical discourse analysis, he argues that issues of interpretative bias emerge. In his view, grounded theory offers corpus linguistics a rigorous methodology for conducting qualitative research, enhancing coding practices and theoretical abstractions. His work, therefore, issues a call for greater engagement between corpus and grounded theory approaches in qualitative, thematic coding. Responding to this call, this chapter draws together approaches in corpus linguistics (Pérez-Paredes, 2020), grounded theory as conceptualised in Hadley (2017), and Dafouz and Smit's ROAD-MAPPING framework (2016, 2020) to present a novel top-down and bottom-up methodology for analysing socially constructed EMI discourses in interviews and focus groups.

4.3 Proposed methodology: corpus linguistics, grounded theory and ROAD-MAPPING

This section presents a brief overview of the ROAD-MAPPING framework, in Section 4.3.1, and grounded theory and the corpus linguistics approach: keyword analysis, in Section 4.3.2 with a view to presenting a combined corpus linguistics, grounded theory and ROAD-MAPPING approach in Section 4.3.3.

4.3.1 The ROAD-MAPPING framework

ROAD-MAPPING is a theoretical framework, developed by Dafouz and Smit (2016, 2020), that affords the analysis of the social and discursive construction of a set of EMEMUS dimensions. The framework spans six dimensions that are drawn from sociolinguistics, ecolinguistics, and language policy research (Dafouz & Smit, 2020). These dimensions are as follows: Roles of English (RO), Academic Disciplines (AD), Language Management (M), the Role of the Agents (A), Practices and Processes (PP) and, finally, Internationalisation and Glocalisation (ING). In using ROAD-MAPPING to analyse interviews, each dimension must be understood in its complexity.

Following Dafouz and Smit (2016, 2020), the RO dimension can help to identify discourse that constructs the perceived position of English in higher education language planning, roles of other languages and role of multilingual policies. It can also be used to identify discourse that sees English as the main language of dissemination of scientific ideas and an increasingly relevant language of education, discourses of English proficiency, programme entry requirements, language gatekeeping, and discourses surrounding English for Specific/Academic Purposes, English as a Lingua Franca, and English for communication, for example.

For AD, the implementation of programmes in EMEMUS challenges previous beliefs and practices in mainstream academic literacies by way of engaging in new norms, values, and ways of constructing knowledge. Therefore, AD can be used to identify and unpack discourses related to academic disciplines, epistemologies, literacies, and acculturation and socialisation, for example. It can also serve to identify discourses related to specific genres, assessment formats, inter- and transdisciplinarity, and the anglocentric monocultural model potentially triggered by the use of English as the language of instruction.

M considers the variety of policies that, at different levels, regulate and manipulate the use of languages in higher education. It can be used to locate and categorise discourses related to managerial decisions, agents, regulations, policies, and multilingual practices, for example. Overlapping with M, A can be used to identify discourses surrounding individual and institutional agents that impact the implementation of programmes in EMEMUS. These include teachers, students, administrative staff, and faculties. This dimension also considers the role of content and language teachers, and the role of hierarchies in determining and shaping agency.

For PP, the dimension understands social practices as cultural conceptions concerned with the administrative, research, and educational activities that construct and are constructed by EMEMUS. This considers ways of doing and thinking, classroom practices, teachers' beliefs and teachers' activities. The final dimension, ING, considers discourses spanning synergies and tensions in internationalisation and glocalisation, including ways to internationalise, staff mobility, international and domestic students, mono/multilingualism, and curricula, for example.

Given its breadth, the ROAD-MAPPING frameworks offer a comprehensive means to capture and categorise EMEMUS and EMI discourses. However, applying these dimensions from a top-down perspective is not without its challenges. Dafouz and Smit identify overlap between the dimensions, which they argue as strength of the framework. However, making sense of this overlap requires 'a detailed account of the dimensions and their theoretical take' in order for the dimensions to become 'truly operative and useful' (Dafouz & Smit, 2020, p. 140). Arguably, using grounded theory and corpus linguistics approaches would support the operationalisation of the framework, given their aforementioned systematicity and rigour. Therefore, the following section considers how grounded theory and the corpus linguistics method of keyword and key term analysis can support such an endeavour.

4.3.2 *Grounded theory and keyword analysis*

Following Hadley (2017), grounded theory allows for a focus on actions and social processes that are transferrable across similar social or educational environments. As a methodology, grounded theory is reflexive, with no set epistemological and ontological positioning (Mills et al., 2006). The coding process fractures the data, moving beyond a linear perspective of the data collected and the coding is iterative, allowing for the mutual shaping of codes by one another as they emerge (Hadley, 2017). Overall, grounded theory affords the development and interrogation of theoretical perspectives, moving beyond empirical paradigms.[1]

Employing grounded theory necessitates an openness to emerging codes from the data and a system of moving from open field codes to more focused codes that pertain to a core category. Such an approach can allow for a deep understanding of the complexity and nuance underpinning macro themes evident in the data being studied. Procedurally, grounded theory involves tagging data with open field, focused, and core codes, the latter of which, in the case of this study, pertains to ROAD-MAPPING codes. Open field codes are bottom-up codes that the researcher observes as emerging from the data, ROAD-MAPPING core categories are top-down codes pertaining to Roles of English, Academic Discipline, Language Management, Agents, Practices and Processes and Internationalisation and Glocalisation, and focused codes are a bridge between these two sets of codes (e.g., Hu & Lei, 2014). In this context, we used corpus linguistics to afford the generation of field codes (Hadley, 2017) by using keyword analysis.

Simply put, keyword analysis involves comparing the (often specialised) corpus being analysed with a reference corpus, which typically represents a balanced collection of comparable language. The aim of such a comparison is to set in relief the language in the corpus being analysed that is notably frequent or salient when compared to the reference corpus as well as the language that can be said to be characteristic of the corpus data, that is, its 'aboutness' (Scott, 2010). Using complex statistical methods (Baron et al., 2009), tools such as AntConc (Anthony, 2022) and Sketch Engine (Kilgarriff et al., 2014) offer a flexible means to compute keywords and, in the case of Sketch Engine, key terms—multiword key items.[2] A noteworthy alignment between corpus linguistics keyword analysis and grounded theory is the shared value of keywords and key terms, and open field codes to describe what is occurring in the text analysed (Hadley, 2017), that is the aboutness of the text (Scott, 2010). Therefore, there is a clear affordance to merge these approaches as a means to fracture the texts and coding process and offer a non-linear avenue into the data.

4.3.3 Combining corpus linguistics, grounded theory, and ROAD-MAPPING

Bringing together keyword analysis, a grounded theory analytical framework, and the ROAD-MAPPING conceptual framework, this chapter proposes the following methodology that can be used to systematically and critically analyse EMI-themed interviews and focus groups, and arguably wider EMI discourses. First, the interviews and focus groups are transcribed following 'intelligent' verbatim transcription processes (i.e., the likes of fillers and hesitations were not transcribed; Hickley, 2007). The interviews and focus groups are parsed at the level of the turn, where turns can be understood as utterances bound by the changing of speakers (Drew, 2004). Organising the discourse by turn allows for the identification of the multiple sites in which ROAD-MAPPING dimensions are socially constructed. Given that there is no consensus on how interviews can or should be theorised in applied linguistics (Talmy & Richards, 2011), the decision to focus on the turn is also underpinned by a corpus linguistics perspective, which places emphasis on usage and how variation in usage reveals attitudes and ideologies towards reality.

Second, a bottom-up approach is applied to the data, attributing field and focus codes to the discourse. To identify and apply field codes, keyword analysis is used. By comparing the corpus of interviews and focus groups with the enTenTen20[3] corpus (Kilgarriff et al., 2014), a number of relevant keywords and key terms are produced. These keywords and key terms (e.g., Spanish, English, and bilingual group) are then annotated to each turn in which they occur. As an initial way into the data, these keywords serve two purposes. First, they signal the turns in which the target discourse is constructed, and second, they highlight the words in these turns worthy of attention and around which EMEMUS/EMI themed discourse is constructed.

Third, from a top-down perspective, the ROAD-MAPPING codes (RO/AD/M/A/PP/ING) are applied to all turns annotated with open field codes. It is likely that some turns contain multiple ROAD-MAPPING codes. This annotation results in a comprehensive overview of the aspects of the discourse that correspond to the ROAD-MAPPING dimensions. However, given the breadth of these dimensions for categorising relevant discourses, focused codes are needed to make sense of and truly operationalise the ROAD-MAPPING framework.

Fourth, focused codes are applied to all turns with field and ROAD-MAPPING codes. This is done by using the 58 focused codes identified by drawing on Dafouz and Smit (2016) (see Pérez-Paredes & Curry, 2022 for the comprehensive list). The following exemplify these focused codes:

- ***RO1*** Position of English in higher education language planning.
- ***AD1*** Academic disciplines.
- ***M1*** Language management statements (vary in terms of range of application and legal status).
- ***A1*** Institutional actors.
- ***PP1*** Ways of doing.
- ***ING1*** Different ways to internationalise (abroad, at home, intl. of the curriculum).

During steps three and four, to ensure coding consistency, a form of inter/intra-rater agreement testing is required. For example, Stemler's (2004) consensus estimates are effective in combination with grounded theory, given the focus on iterative coding development and agreement.

The final step involves the analysis of the interviews and focus groups by drawing on field, focused, and ROAD-MAPPING codes, as well as the wider context. In analysing the data, first, the occurrence of all ROAD-MAPPING codes is identified to demonstrate which dimensions are present in the data. Second, ROAD-MAPPING profiles of each interview and focus group are created based on the comprehensive open field and focused coding process, with a view to identifying shared patterns and idiosyncrasies in EMI lecturers' discursive construction of ROAD-MAPPING and EMEMUS/EMI.

4.4 Case study

Building on previous work on the Agents, and Practices and Process dimensions (Curry & Pérez-Paredes, 2021) and Internationalisation and Glocalisation dimension (Pérez-Paredes & Curry, 2022), this brief case study adds to these findings a focus on the Roles of English guided by the following research questions:

- How is the RO dimension discursively constructed by EMI lecturers in the data analysed?
- What can a combined use of corpus linguistics approaches, grounded theory, and ROAD-MAPPING afford research on EMI?

To answer these questions, the methodology outlined in Section 4.3.3 is applied to the data presented in Section 4.4.1. Subsequently, Section 4.4.2 briefly presents and discusses the findings of the analysis, primarily as a means to illustrate the methodology. It should be noted that this case study is necessarily brief and serves largely to illustrate the affordances of the methodology described in Section 4.3.3. More comprehensive analyses of ROAD-MAPPING dimensions in the data described herein are available in Curry and Pérez-Paredes (2021) and Pérez-Paredes and Curry (2022).

4.4.1 Data and method

The data used in this study have been analysed in Curry and Pérez-Paredes (2021) and Pérez-Paredes and Curry (2022) and are composed of five semi-structured interviews and two focus groups with EMI lecturers in a Spanish EMEMUS. Table 4.1 presents key, descriptive information for each recording.

As these are semi-structured interviews, each lecturer was encouraged to dig deeply into their reflections, which afforded critical engagement with their EMI practices. The questions they were asked are presented in the Appendix. Furthermore, in Interview 1, there are two participants, owing to the participants' availability. The inclusion of two participants in this interview has not impacted its quality, as participants spoke openly, sharing corresponding

Table 4.1 Interview and focus group details

	Code	Discipline	Length in minutes: minutes	Word count	No. of participants
Interview 1	I1	Business & history	29:33	5046	2
Interview 2	I2	Law	26:21	4754	1
Interview 3	I3	Education	33:18	5256	1
Interview 4	I4	Biology	28:15	5013	1
Interview 5	I5	Physical sciences	27:11	4743	1
Focus Group 1	FG1	Multidisciplinary	57:55	9343	9
Focus Group 2	FG2	Multidisciplinary	55:12	8974	9

Table 4.2 Top 10 keywords and key terms (field codes)

Keywords	Key terms
bilingual	bilingual programme
Spanish	bilingual group
Erasmus	academic language
English	transactional language
Lingua	language teaching
EMI	face-to-face stuff
pedagogy	international context
franca	language centre
Kahoot!	language education
transactional	English level

and diverging views based on their individual experiences, disciplines, and contexts. For Focus Groups 1 and 2, there were different foci and the questions for each are presented in the Appendix. Each focus group included nine participants and the participants came from the following disciplines: Business Economics, Law, Primary Education, New Technologies in Computer Sciences, Physical Sciences, and Biology. After the interviews and focus groups were transcribed, they were prepared for manual annotation and analysis.

In applying the method outlined in Section 4.3.3 to these data, for each step the following relevant data were identified:

1 Across all seven recordings, 1,390 turns were identified.
2 A total of 84 EMI-related keywords and 31 EMI-related key terms were identified when the data were compared with the enTenTen20 corpus using Sketch Engine (Kilgarriff et al., 2014). See Table 4.2 for the top 10 keywords and key terms extracted. All the keywords and key terms were used as open field codes and were applied to 229 and 99 turns, respectively.
3 A total of 739 ROAD-MAPPING were applied to these turns and those surrounding turns tagged with keywords and key terms.

4 A total of 835 focused codes were applied to turns containing ROAD-MAPPING and open field codes. Focused codes are drawn from the comprehensive list presented in Pérez-Paredes and Curry (2022).
5 Stemler's (2004) consensus estimates were used to iteratively and collaboratively develop the coding process. Upon completion, 20% of the codes were reviewed to ensure agreement and consistency in coding practices.
6 The data were analysed based on this coding process.

4.4.2 Results and discussion

Overall, the RO code is the most frequent core category applied to the data, accounting for 28% of the instances in which the discourse centred on EMEMUS/EMI across the data, as presented in Table 4.3. Furthermore, across the interviews and focus groups, RO is the most frequent code in I1, I2, FG1 and FG2, the second most frequent code in I3 and I5, and the third most frequent code in I4. The prevalence of this code reflects the view that lecturers need to understand the role of English in their teaching practice in EMEMUS (Dearden, 2018).

Unpacking the RO code further, it appears to co-occur with a number of other ROAD-MAPPING codes. Two of the most common co-occurring codes are PP and A. Example (1) reflects RO through the lecturer's act of gatekeeping student intake by commenting on their need to rise to the challenge if they are to succeed (Dafouz & Smit, 2020). This co-occurs with their reflections on PP as 'ways of doing' and is signalled by the keywords and key terms in bold.

(1) As well as I am investing in my convention in **English**, so they need to improve their **English**, they have to work on that. I can provide **lectures**; I am happy to provide **explanations** for economical concepts and economic history **classes**, but I'm not going to go further. Actually, I refuse to do checks and to ask for **essays** in my **subject**, because I'm not going to do that.

(I1)

Table 4.3 Distribution of ROAD-MAPPING codes across the data

ROAD-MAPPING code	Overall count	%	I1%	I2%	I3%	I4%	I5%	FG1%	FG2%
RO	204	28	33	26	24	16	24	38	32
PP	195	26	16	15	43	36	25	22	23
A	118	16	22	23	11	4	12	21	18
AD	88	12	16	12	9	11	16	9	15
ING	100	13	8	19	3	23	22	7	12
M	34	5	5	4	11	10	0	3	0
Total	**739**	**100**	**100**	**100**	**100**	**100**	**100**	**100**	**100**

In Example (2), RO is realised through the discussion of English with other languages, and the value of English for communication and as lingua franca of higher education. Again, RO co-occurs with other ROAD-MAPPING codes, A in this case, as there is an overlap between the development of English language competency, the acquisition of academic literacy for learners, and a vision of their socialisation into academic communities of practice (Dafouz & Smit, 2020). Again, the keywords in bold signal the words that surfaced this utterance as a site in which EMI discourse was constructed.

> (2) My case it's a little bit more **different**, because I come from computer science. So they read a lot of books in **English**, because the **terminology** is in **English**. . . . So sometimes they are in **Spanish**, so if you don't want to do anything in **English** you can go there; but if you go to the, for example, the place where I'm **teaching**, it's completely in **English** so they know where they are going to. So usually my role there is I'm trying to get them familiarised with the concepts, but, in my point of view, I'm not trying to **teach** them any **English**. If they are able to understand me, that's good, just that.
>
> (FG1)

Another perspective afforded by this approach is the interrogation of focused codes. Table 4.4 presents the presence of RO focused codes in the data as well as their brief explanation.

Unpacking Table 4.4, it is clear that RO1 and RO4 are the most common themes that emerge, exemplified in Example (3), with keywords in bold.

> (3) My line of research is basically developing this in **English**, although in **Spanish**, of course. I am also vice-chair of Action Cost, and lead a research **programme**. So I have to be—keep pushing up my English constantly, because I realised that to **talk** is okay, and everybody is nice with you. But if you have to go deeper in a topic you really need these skills, and you have to be polite and you need a level of **English** that, otherwise, they will be excluded from the really important conversations.
>
> (I1)

In Example (3), RO is made evident by the lecturer in terms of both research and teaching, demonstrating that in the EMEMUS context, lecturers engagement with English is motivated by a number of different factors, such as career in this case (Volchenkova & Kravtsova, 2021).

Overall, this is quite a brief review and largely serves to illustrate the methodology. However, in reflecting on the question of how the RO dimension is discursively constructed by EMI lecturers, the methodology makes clear that this theme is influenced and influences other dimensions and is flexibly constructed, evidenced in the range of focused codes that denote

Table 4.4 RO focused codes across the data

Focused codes		Count	Percentage of all focused codes	Percentage of RO focused codes
RO1	Position of English in higher education language planning	65	8	23
RO2	Roles of other languages (foreign, national, regional, minority or migrant languages)	33	4	12
RO3	Multilingual policies	5	1	2
RO4	English as the main language of dissemination of scientific ideas and an increasingly relevant language of education	62	7	22
RO5	Proof of English proficiency	3	0	1
RO6	Entry requirements for EMI programmes	10	1	4
RO7	Gatekeeper regulating (non-native) student intake	23	3	8
RO8	Staff's proficiency level (as a necessity for teaching in EM programmes)	14	2	5
RO9	Educational aims linked to future professional language requirements	7	1	2
RO10	English for specific purposes classes	1	0	0
RO11	Outcomes criterion	0	0	0
RO12	Coursework (as a subject in English for academic purposes classes, as means of teaching and learning)	2	0	1
RO13	English can be drawn on in relation to some or all communicative skills	31	4	11
RO14	Lingua franca of many higher educational settings	27	3	10
Total		**283**	**34**	**100**

Source: Adapted from Pérez-Paredes & Curry, 2022.

the thematic reach of the RO dimension. The main findings presented demonstrate that RO co-occurs with PP and A (also discussed in Curry & Pérez-Paredes, 2021) and largely draws on career-oriented reflections of the value and role of English. To respond to the second research question, investigating the affordances of a combined use of corpus linguistics approaches, grounded theory, and ROAD-MAPPING to conduct research on EMI, we argue that the systematic approach to identifying open field codes as keywords and key terms allows for the identification, in a lateral, non-linear fashion, of key sites in discourse in which perceptions of EMI are socially constructed by the lecturers.

4.5 Conclusions

The combined use of keyword analysis, grounded theory, and ROAD-MAPPING presents EMI researchers with exciting opportunities to examine interview and focus group data, as well as other texts in which EMEMUS/EMI discourses are socially constructed. The methodology discussed in Section 4.3.3, far from decontextualising the emerging themes in the interviews, creates the conditions for a careful examination and comparison of how *themes* are discursively constructed and how lexical items contribute to such construction. The role of frequency and language use for unpacking the meanings people ascribe to ideas and objects needs further attention in social and education research (Pérez-Paredes, 2020). Our methodology seeks to contribute to this effort.

As McEnery and Brezina (2022) note, a corpus represents an amalgam of social and physical interactions. The examination of such interactions through the lens of keywords and key terms can complement the use of other analytical frameworks such as ROAD-MAPPING, which researchers may consider fit to facilitate their interpretation of data. The use of grounded theory to create a bridge (Hu & Lei, 2014) between the bottom-up 'aboutness' of keywords and the top-down categorisation of ROAD-MAPPING dimensions offers a pathway for operationalising the ROAD-MAPPING framework (Dafouz & Smit, 2020). Moreover, this approach reinforces and supports the view that corpus linguistics can inform a systematic view of mixed-methods research (Hashemi, 2019).

We, as corpus linguists, are influenced by the epistemological practices in our discipline, which hold that social sciences should 'actively seek and maximise the potential for falsification' (McEnery & Brezina, 2022, p. 253). We would like to see the proposed methodology as an application of corpus-informed textual analysis methods to qualitative research in that 'depth of meaning and people's subjective experiences and their meaning-making processes' (Leavy, 2017, p. 124) remain central to the methodology.

Notes

1 Much more could be said about grounded theory. However, there is not space enough here to consider it in detail. See Hadley (2017) for a detailed account of grounded theory and its relevance/applicability to applied linguistics and education research.
2 For a detailed, step-by-step introduction to keyword analysis, see Pérez-Paredes (2020).
3 The enTenTen20 corpus is an English corpus made up of texts collected from the Internet. It is produced by Sketch Engine (Kilgarriff et al., 2014) and totals 36 billion words.

References

Aijmer, K., & Rühlemann, C. (Eds.). (2015). *Corpus pragmatics*. Cambridge University Press.

Anthony, L. (2022). *AntConc (Version 4.1.2)* [Computer software]. Waseda University. www.laurenceanthony.net/software

Baron, A., Rayson, P., & Archer, D. (2009). Word frequency and key word statistics in corpus linguistics. *Anglistik, 20*(1), 41–67.

Chang, S. Y. (2019). Beyond the English box: Constructing and communicating knowledge through translingual practices in the higher education classroom. *English Teaching & Learning, 43*(1), 23–40.

Curry, N. (2022). Question illocutionary force indicating devices in academic writing: A corpus-pragmatic and contrastive approach to identifying and analysing direct and indirect questions in English, French, and Spanish. *International Journal of Corpus Linguistics, 28*(1), 91–119.

Curry, N., & Pérez-Paredes, P. (2021). Understanding lecturers' practices and processes: An investigation of English medium education in a Spanish multilingual university. In M. L. Carrió-Pastor & B. Bellés Fortuño (Eds.), *Teaching language and content in multicultural and multilingual classrooms: CLIL and EMI approaches* (pp. 123–156). Palgrave Macmillan.

Dafouz, E., & Smit, U. (2016). Towards a dynamic conceptual framework for English-medium education in multilingual university settings. *Applied Linguistics, 37*(3), 397–415.

Dafouz, E., & Smit, U. (2020). *Road-mapping English medium education in the internationalised university*. Palgrave Macmillan.

Dearden, J. (2018). The changing roles of EMI academics and English language specialists. In Y. Kırkgöz & K. Dikilitaş (Eds.), *Key issues in English for specific purposes in higher education* (pp. 323–338). Springer.

Drew, P. (2004). Conversation analysis. In K. L. Fitch & R. E. Sanders (Eds.), *Handbook of language and social interaction* (pp. 71–102). Psychology Press.

Erkan, A., & Dikilitaş, K. (2022). Turkish undergraduates' perspectives on EMI: A framework induced analysis of policies and processes. In Y. Kirkgöz & A. Karakaş (Eds.), *English as the medium of instruction in Turkish higher education* (pp. 135–153). Springer.

Galloway, N., Numajiri, T., & Rees, N. (2020). The "internationalisation", or "Englishisation", of higher education in East Asia. *Higher Education, 80*(3), 395–414.

Hadley, G. (2017). *Grounded theory in applied linguistics research: A practical guide*. Routledge.

Hashemi, M. R. (2019). Expanding the scope of mixed methods research in applied linguistics. In J. McKinley & H. Rose (Eds.), *The Routledge handbook of research methods in applied linguistics* (pp. 39–51). Routledge.

Hickley, A. (2007). Finding affordable transcription for research interviews. *Ezine @rticles* [online]. Available: https://ezinearticles.com/?Finding-Affordable-Transcription-for-Research-Interviews&id=473893. Last accessed 13 April 2023.

Hu, G., & Lei, J. (2014). English-medium instruction in Chinese higher education: A case study. *Higher Education, 67*(5), 551–567.

Huang, W., & Fang, F. (2022). EMI Teachers' perceptions and practices regarding culture teaching in Chinese higher education. *Language, Culture and Curriculum*, 1–17.

Jon, J. E., Cho, Y. H., & Byun, K. (2020). Internationalization by English-medium instruction? Professors' decoupling behaviors to EMI policy in Korean higher education. *KEDI Journal of Educational Policy, 17*(2), 297–318.

Kilgarriff, A., Baisa, V., Bušta, J., Jakubíček, M., Kovář, V., Michelfeit, J., Rychlý, P., & Suchomel, V. (2014). The Sketch Engine: Ten years on. *Lexicography, 1*, 7–36.

King, N., Horrocks, C., & Brooks, J. (2018). *Interviews in qualitative research.* Sage.

Larzen-Ostermark, E. (2008). The intercultural dimension in EFL-teaching: A study of conceptions among Finland-Swedish comprehensive school teachers. *Scandinavian Journal of Educational Research, 52*(5), 527–547. https://doi.org/10.1080/00313830802346405

Leavy, P. (2017). *Research design: Quantitative, qualitative, mixed methods, arts-based, and community-based participatory research approaches.* Guilford Publications.

Martel, J., & Wang, A. (2014). Language teacher identity. In M. Bigelow & J. Ennser-Kananen (Eds.), *The Routledge handbook of educational linguistics* (pp. 311–322). Routledge.

McEnery, T., & Brezina, V. (2022). *Fundamental principles of corpus linguistics.* Cambridge University Press.

Mills, J., Bonner, A., & Francis, K. (2006). The development of constructivist grounded theory. *International Journal of Qualitative Methods, 5*(1), 25–35.

O'Halloran, K. (2014). Corpus linguistics. In C. Leung & B. V. Street (Eds.), *The Routledge companion to English studies* (pp. 288–303). Routledge.

Pérez-Paredes, P. (2020). *Corpus linguistics for education. A guide for research.* Routledge.

Pérez-Paredes, P., & Curry, N. (2022). Exploring the internationalization and glocalization constructs in EMEMUS lecturers interviews and focus groups. In U. Smit & E. Dafouz (Eds.), *English-medium education across multilingual university settings: Applications and critical evaluations of the ROAD-MAPPING framework.* Routledge.

Saldaña, J. (2013). *The coding manual for qualitative researchers* (2nd ed.). Sage.

Scott, M. (2010). Problems in investigating keyness, or clearing the undergrowth and marking out trails. In M. Bondi & M. Scott (Eds.), *Keyness in texts* (pp. 43–57). John Benjamins Publishing Company.

Sinclair, J. (2004). *Trust the text: Language, corpus and discourse.* Routledge.

Spolsky, B. (2009). *Language management.* Cambridge University Press.

Stemler, S. E. (2004). A comparison of consensus, consistency, and measurement approaches to estimating interrater reliability. *Practical Assessment, Research, and Evaluation, 9*(1), 1–11.

Talmy, S., & Richards, K. (2011). Theorizing qualitative research interviews in applied linguistics. *Applied Linguistics, 32*(1), 1–5.

Volchenkova, K., & Kravtsova, E. (2021). EMI lecturer trainers: Reflections on the implementation of EMI lecturer training course. *Alicante Journal of English Studies/ Revista Alicantina de Estudios Ingleses: RAEI, 34*, 185–219.

Appendix

For each interview, participants were asked about:

- Their use and engagement with English, both professionally and in everyday life.
- Their views on teaching in English and Spanish.
- The roles of content and language in their teaching.
- Their perceptions of their students' feelings about studying in English.
- Their opinions on differences between academic English and academic Spanish.
- The role of technology in their EMEMUS practices.

For the focus groups, there were two different foci. Focus Group 1 was concerned with the role of language in EMEMUS and questions and prompts pertained to:

- The roles of lecturers in EMEMUS.
- Their views on language use.
- Learner language.
- Language challenges.
- The role of the first language.
- The use of language technology in their EMEMUS practices.

Focus Group 2 centred on pedagogy and questions asked the group to reflect on:

- Their EMEMUS pedagogies;
- The differences between teaching in English and Spanish;
- Their approaches to EMEMUS instruction;
- Their understanding of EMEMUS students' needs;
- Their own staff development needs; and
- Their use of educational technology.

5 Affordances of conversation analysis for investigating EMI classroom talk

Reka R. Jablonkai

5.1 Introduction

Conversation analysis (CA) originates as an approach in sociology from an interest in the function of language as a means for social interaction. Early representatives of this approach proposed to examine and analyse social interaction through detailed observation of actual conversations occurring naturally. In CA there is a clear focus and interest in social action and concern with people's 'lived experiences' (Sacks et al., 1974). As such CA falls under the qualitative research paradigm that aims to understand, describe and explain social phenomena by analysing experiences, documents and interactions primarily with an emic (insider) approach from the participants' perspective (Silverman, 2016; Rapley, 2008). Conversation analysts consider talk as action and focus on what participants *do* in their talk in social situations and processes which can include mundane activities, for example invitations, dating, doctor–patient interactions and legal hearings (Richard & Seedhouse, 2005, p. xviii). Although the origins of CA go back to an approach in sociology, its concern with language-in-use made it a widely used and recognised approach in applied linguistics. CA studies extended our understanding of language use in contexts of second-language acquisition (Markee, 2005; Seedhouse et al., 2010), language classrooms (Seedhouse, 2004; Walsh, 2011; Wong & Waring, 2010) and study abroad (Wilkinson, 1998), for example.

A CA methodology involves a bottom-up, data-driven approach to analysis. Conversation analysts examine recordings of conversations, institutional talk and naturally occurring interactions by paying close attention to the transcripts that include details of verbal and multimodal (e.g. gaze, gesture and pause) means of the interaction. This microanalytic and inductive stance to talk and attention to turn-taking, repair and sequencing offers conversation analysts a way into the ordered infrastructure of human interaction and participants' competencies, goals and understandings (Silverman, 2016).

The role of conversation is also foregrounded in sociocultural theories of learning (Vygotsky, 1978). Research into dialogic pedagogies and second-language acquisition supports the view that classroom interaction as a form

Affordances of conversation analysis for investigating EMI 63

of conversation is at the centre of all learning and effective teaching (Mercer, 2000; Thornbury & Slade, 2006). The majority of previous CA research on classroom talk and interaction was conducted in school contexts (e.g. Dalton-Puffer, 2007) and language learning classrooms (e.g. Seedhouse, 2004; Walsh, 2011). There is, however, a dearth of CA research into classroom talk and conversational interaction in higher education contexts in general and in EMI educational contexts in particular. This paucity is especially disconcerting as (1) students' engagement in classroom interaction has been found crucial in developing disciplinary knowledge, (2) small group discussion is a widely used element in higher education pedagogy and (3) therefore students spend a considerable amount of time in educational settings where they are expected to interact (Heron & Dippold, 2021). Furthermore, EMI university classes are often multilingual and multicultural learning contexts with reported challenges for students and teachers (Curle et al., 2020; Dang & Vu, 2020). Although frameworks to promote interaction for learning have been proposed (Arkoudis et al., 2013), a better understanding of the interactional dynamics of such classrooms is needed to effectively plan, support and create environments for interaction for learning. A CA methodology is well-situated to answer questions relating to the effective interactional dynamics of teaching. The present chapter will discuss the foundations and basic steps of applying a CA methodology and the dimensions of higher education classroom talk that could especially benefit from harnessing the affordances of a CA approach.

5.2 Strengths and potential focus of a CA approach to EMI classroom talk

Researchers demonstrated several strengths of a CA approach compared to other frameworks for analysing talk in action. They highlight that a CA methodology:

(a) Is concerned with naturally occurring interactions and is strictly empirical and data-driven. Researchers aim to identify patterns that emerge from the data without bringing preconceived categories to the data.
(b) Aims to offer an emic (insider) perspective by attempting to give an account of the interaction through the lens of the participants.
(c) Is concerned with the sequential organisation of the interaction as constructed by the participants and the context in which the interaction takes place.
(d) Views talk in institutional settings as goal-oriented, that is, participants pursue objectives that are related to the institution. In an EMI classroom, for example, classroom talk is influenced by the institutional goals of subject-specific content and language learning outcomes (Seedhouse, 2004; Silverman, 2016; ten Have, 2007; Walsh, 2011).

This chapter argues that these strengths allow CA to provide nuanced insight into the talk and interaction in the multilingual and multicultural EMI classrooms. The main areas where EMI research can harness the affordances of a microanalytic CA approach are (1) the analysis of teacher–student and student–student interaction; (2) the analysis of 'doing explanations'; and (3) the analysis of the roles and uses of multiple languages. In what follows these three broad areas are discussed.

5.2.1 Teacher–student and student–student interaction

Early analysis of classroom talk described a recurring pattern often abbreviated as IRE/F (Mehan, 1979; Sinclair & Coulthard, 1975). In this recurring triad, the teacher initiates (I) a question, a selected student responds (R) and the teacher evaluates or follows up (E/F) on the student's response. Linguistic and educational studies demonstrated how this interaction pattern reflects the asymmetrical roles teachers and students assume as teachers control classroom talk by asking questions, setting agendas, selecting students and evaluating responses. Jacknick and Duran (2021), for example, focus on the teacher's third turn to demonstrate how the turn is used to orient students to subject-specific terms and knowledge. They found that the teacher in an EMI Educational Sciences course in Turkey accomplished a number of interrelated actions in the I/F turn including modelling how to be a teacher, familiarising students with disciplinary terminology as well as inviting students to imagine themselves as part of an expert community. To this end, the teacher deploys a wide range of linguistic and multimodal resources. For example, she used the pronoun 'we' to include students in the community of experts, she used gaze and gesture to orient to students who made a contribution and moved around in the classroom or positioned herself to shift between focusing on one student and inviting the group of students to respond.

More recent analyses suggest a shift in the strictly asymmetrical interactional dynamics of classroom talk. Benwell and Stokoe (2002), for example, observed that tutors when setting tasks in tutorials at British universities deploy a three-part sequence with the following functions of each part: (a) future projection of the task: for example *I thought we could go over (2.0) some of the questions*; (b) contextual details to express and justify the limits of the task optionally including reference to past actions: for example *we've done the interactions of charged particles we've done the interactions of gamma rays and we've done (.) a little bit on neutrons*; and (c) orienting to immediate next action that often invites students to participate: *you can tell me (0.4) all about phasars now (.) OK? (0.2) who's going to start* (p. 434). The authors suggest that such three-part sequences do not only serve a regulative function to control and set the task but also pursue a more 'democratic' approach where interactional power is negotiated. The second part in the sequence, especially, may reflect an attempt to provide transparency regarding the aims and justification of the task. This part often included extensive contextual details, which may function to prepare students for contributing to the tutorial and to manage face-work (Goffman, 1967).

In an EMI context, Duran and Sert (2021) examined student-initiated questions in the Turkish higher education. The authors focused on multi-unit questions with the following basic pattern:

(1) A pre-sequence (Can I ask a question?).
(2) A wh-interrogative question (What was the difference between consulting and counselling?).
(3) An extended teacher turn + Understanding check (Okay?).
(4) Student marked acknowledgement (Okay, nodding) (p. 1).

They demonstrated how students use background statements, prefaces and multiple questions often to initiate new topics that were not dealt with indicating learner agency. The teacher manages these questions and provides multi-unit turns with detailed responses. As a result, these questions offer co-constructed learning opportunities and demonstrate learner agency.

There are only a handful of studies that investigated student–student interaction in classroom talk through a CA lens, despite the affordances of this analytical framework. Stokoe (2000) demonstrated the usefulness of a conversation analytic approach to classroom talk by exploring topic development in small group discussions. She found that students in the opening sequences of small group discussions decided on appropriacy, relevance and legitimacy of topics including 'clarification talk' in which relevance was checked against the instructions and tutor's words in topic-initial sequences. Often what students deemed relevant differed in individual groups. Similar patterns were revealed in the analysis of 'off-topic' episodes during discussions. She concluded that the microanalytic lens of CA that embraces the participants' perspective in interaction offers a nuanced understanding of educational talk. Findings of studies that investigated classroom talk in higher education contexts also underline the importance of a CA approach. Hardman (2016, 2021) in the British higher education context, for example, found that despite the small-group teaching format, educational talk was still primarily teacher-led and the aim of interactions was predominantly to check students' knowledge of the content provided by the teacher. This type of teaching often results in students, especially international students, being silent in the classroom.

A closer look at student–student interaction in small-group discussions with a CA approach also revealed how some students, often international students in Anglophone higher education contexts, become marginalised. Sohn and Spiliotopoulos (2021), for example, used turn-taking analysis and Goffman's participation framework (1974, 1981) to investigate student–student interaction in small-group discussions in the Canadian higher education context. The authors found that international students with developing English proficiency were excluded from the conversation and were marginalised spatially. This was all the more disappointing as the original intention of the teachers was to create an inclusive environment and to provide opportunities for interaction to integrate students from diverse linguistic and cultural backgrounds by group discussions and tasks.

This brief review of CA studies into classroom interaction demonstrated how a CA methodology can provide a nuanced understanding of the interactional dynamics and instructional consequences of particular choices of linguistic and multimodal resources. EMI research with a CA approach could extend our knowledge of the interactional architecture underlying the reported challenges of EMI teachers and students.

5.2.2 Doing explanations in classroom talk

Explaining content and defining terminology and disciplinary vocabulary make up a considerable amount of lecture time. Flowerdew (1992), for example, found that a term is defined every one minute and 55 seconds on average in science lectures. Disciplinary vocabulary encapsulates disciplinary concepts and thus their explanation can provide access to conceptual knowledge (Green & Lambert, 2019; Malström et al., 2017). Students 'doing explanations' have also been demonstrated to promote learning and studies have found that the more complex the explanation the stronger the association with learning (Webb et al., 2009).

Conversation analytic frameworks can shed light on how conceptual knowledge is co-constructed through interaction and what methodological choices are made about explanations and how this linguistic function is organised sequentially in the flow of classroom discourse (Koole, 2010; Llinares & Morton, 2010; Mortensen, 2011; Morton, 2015). There are only a handful of studies that have investigated this aspect of classroom discourse and they were mostly conducted in language teaching or CLIL school contexts (Chaudron, 1982; Markee, 1995; Mortensen, 2011; Morton, 2015; Waring et al., 2013).

Koole (2010), for example, analysed explanations in secondary school maths classes in the Netherlands. He identified two sequential organisations of explanations: discourse unit organisation and dialogue organisation. In the case of discourse unit organisations, the teacher tells the student how to proceed to solve a mathematical problem and uses questions to check understanding. In a dialogue organisation sequence the teacher asks the students questions similar to the IRE (initiation, response, evaluation) format. He also demonstrated how cognitive notions such as 'doing knowing' and 'doing understanding' in the overall action of explanations are used and displayed in interaction. Another study that examined explanations in maths classes focused on students' explanations in the German school context (Heller, 2016). Heller found that access to multimodal resources, for example, pointing to or using objects to demonstrate a mathematical concept (e.g. surface area) while 'doing explanation' has important consequences for the interactional organisation. In her study, the turns of the student who had to rely on verbal resources alone were shorter and did not add new information to the explanation. Both of these studies were conducted in a context where students used their L1, Dutch and German, respectively. Llinares and Morton (2010), however, analysed student explanations in English CLIL classrooms in the Spanish school context. Using a combination of a quantitative corpus-based approach and a qualitative CA approach, the authors compared how students produced explanations in CLIL classroom talk and in an interview situation outside the classroom. Interviewers were found to follow up on students' ideas and display acknowledgement (e.g. by turn-initial 'mm mm') more frequently without evaluation (e.g. by saying 'good'). The authors suggested that the different interactional practices of the teachers and interviewers could be associated with longer turns and more frequent reference to mental, especially cognitive, processes in students' turns (e.g. 'I think', 'I know') in the interview situation. They conclude that heightened self-awareness of CLIL teachers' own interactional practices and the application of interactional practices that are similar to the ones used in the interviews could provide more opportunities for students to produce academic talk such as explanations in classrooms.

An overall description of the sequential organisation of word explanations in language teaching and CLIL classroom talk was provided by Mortensen (2011) and Waring and colleagues (2013). Mortensen (2011) focused on the sequential format of 'doing word explanations' that emerged from the interaction in language teaching classes. He identified the following pattern of such unplanned word explanations:

(a) The teacher emphasises a specific part of the turn.
(b) A student repeats this segment of the turn.
(c) The teacher asks for a word explanation.
(d) The student provides the word explanation (p. 139).

He also discussed the resources the teacher applied to highlight parts of the turn. He found that emphasis was created by a combination of self-repair (Schegloff et al., 1977) and non-verbal resources such as pause, gaze, prolongation of vowels and visual resources using the blackboard. Mortensen's study showed how participants negotiated in their interaction '(a) *that* they initiate a word explanation sequence, (b) *how* they do it, and (c) *which* lexical items are relevant for explanation' (p. 156).

Waring and colleagues (2013) also investigated word explanations in a language teaching context. They offer the following sequence of typical key elements of explanations:

(1) Set WORD in focus (e.g. repeat, display on the board).
(2) Contextualise WORD (e.g. use in a sentence, scene enactment).

(3) Invite (via an understanding-display sequence) or offer an explanation.
(4) Close the explanation with a repetition (e.g. repeat, summarise) (p. 254).

Based on their analysis, Waring and colleagues distinguished between 'analytic' and 'animated' explanations where analytic explanations rely overwhelmingly on verbal resources together with textual resources in the form of providing derivational morphemes, intertextual links and giving definitions with the help of synonyms and paraphrasing. Animated explanations deploy multimodal resources combining verbal and non-verbal, visual and gestural representations. Contextualisation in this sequence is an important addition to the organisation of explanations. It can be done verbally in analytic explanations and by using gestures or acting out in the case of animated explanations. These studies found that gestures were essential elements of word explanations and contributed to the quality of input that students received (Lazaraton, 2004).

Overall, EMI research and practice could benefit from the better understanding of doing content, terminology and word explanations that a CA approach can provide.

5.2.3 Roles and uses of multiple languages

EMI classrooms are multilingual contexts and the role and use of English, L1 and other languages have been the focal point of much of EMI research (Curle et al., 2020). The proportion of classroom talk in EMI classes given in English and L1 shows great variations across geographical areas and is often subject to national or institutional language policies. Classroom observation studies focusing on L1 use suggest that L1 is primarily used for establishing rapport, improving comprehension, explaining subject-specific terminology and providing local examples (e.g. Macaro et al., 2018; Mazak & Herbas-Donoso, 2015; Wang & Curdt-Christiansen, 2019). Although the microanalytic, moment-by-moment analysis of multilingual classroom talk that a CA approach allows to shed light on the role and pedagogical value of codeswitching, translanguaging and code-mixing practices, to date there is a surprising dearth of such research in EMI.

Chen and Bonacina-Pugh (2021) argue that CA is a useful analytical framework and theoretical lens to identify the set of interactional norms and language choice practices that make up what they term 'practiced' language policy. In their analysis of small multilingual student group discussions in a UK higher education, they focus on speakers' response to certain language choices and consider repair and translation sequences as indications of deviant language choice acts that can reveal implicit norms of language choice. They found the different norms adopted in the small groups and the whole classroom interaction depend on the language repertoires of the participants and whether there are shared languages. A CA study by Duran and colleagues (2022) examined students' word search sequences in a Turkish EMI context.

Affordances of conversation analysis for investigating EMI 69

Their findings suggest that such sequences demonstrate how participants construct the EMI language policy in and through their interactions.

Recent research into the use of L1 suggests that students' linguistic repertoires should be embraced and deployed as a resource to support the learning process (Macaro et al., 2018). Using code-switching or translanguaging practices in EMI classroom talk has been found to lead to valuable multilingual pedagogies (Duran et al., 2022; Pun, 2021; Tai, 2021). More CA studies that focus on these practices are therefore needed in order to inform such pedagogies and support teachers to make principled choices regarding the language choices in EMI classroom talk.

5.3 Main stages and steps of doing CA

In general, a CA project can be divided into two main stages: (1) the data collection and preparation and (2) the data analysis stages. As can be seen in Tables 5.1 and 5.2, adapted from guidelines for novice conversation analysts by Pomerantz and Fehr (1997) and ten Have (2007), these stages involve several steps which, however, as is often the case in qualitative methodologies, are intertwined rather than follow a strict linear order (ten Have, 2007). The space in this chapter does not allow for a detailed description of the individual steps, therefore, the main principles will be discussed here. First, conversation analysts investigate 'naturally occurring' interactions which means that researchers aim to observe and record classroom talk in an unobtrusive fashion. This often means setting up several cameras and audio-recorders in the classroom. Examples of how to set up recording devices in the classroom to capture relevant verbal and multimodal resources can be found in the studies given in the third column of Table 5.1. Ethical issues should always be considered and consent of participants needs to be obtained before any recording can be made (Dalton-Puffer, 2007; Rapley, 2008; ten Have, 2007; Walsh, 2011). Sampling needs to be based on the focus of the analysis which might be classroom talk in a particular educational setting or a particular type of interaction (e.g. questions, small group discussions) in the classroom, for example. Second, transcription is a very much interpretative activity. Although CA has a number of transcription conventions to record verbal, multimodal and other details of conversations, during transcription the researcher needs to be selective in what details to represent (Prior & Talmy, 2019).

Third, the data analysis starts with what is termed as an 'unmotivated look' and noticing (ten Have, 2007, p. 121) of the social actions being conducted. This generally means a data-driven approach; that is, analysts should start from the data (the recordings, transcripts) rather than from preconceived concepts. Ten Have (p. 121), however, points out that the analytical concepts and findings accumulated over the five decades of CA tradition should not be ignored and could structure the noticing in more recent CA studies. Investigation of classroom talk can be conducted at several levels. Researchers

Table 5.1 Steps of data collection and preparation for CA

Steps	Considerations	Example studies
Capturing classroom talk	Focus of analysis Making one's own recording or using existing recordings Setting and arrangement Ethical issues	Audio recording Benwell and Stokoe (2002, p. 432) Video recording and set up Duran et al. (2022, pp. 506–507) Duran and Sert (2019, p. 76) Koole (2010, 184) Lazaraton (2004, p. 92)
Sampling	Focus of analysis Size of group Participants in group/class Discipline, year group Educational context	Benwell and Stokoe (2002, p. 432): eight hours of audio recordings of tutorial with three to 10 participants from a range of disciplines to analyse tutor's task formulations Duran and Sert (2019, p. 76): 30 hours of video recordings of EMI university classes to analyse preference organisation
Transcription	Verbal Translation Multimodal Using transcription software	Jefferson (2004) transcription convention Transana Duran and Sert (2019, p. 76) transcription software ELAN (2022) multimodal annotation software

(Adapted from Walsh, 2011; ten Have, 2007, p. 71, 73, 109; Jenks, 2021)

can focus on (1) the overarching activity framework (e.g. participating in tutorials), (2) the sequence of actions (e.g. giving instructions sequence), (3) individual actions (e.g. explanations) and (4) individual features (e.g. lexical choices, silence). The questions and example studies in Table 5.2 give further guidance for interrogating and interpreting classroom talk data.

5.4 Concluding remarks

This brief overview aimed to highlight the affordances of a CA methodology for EMI research. The microanalytic lens, focus on naturally occurring conversations, an analytical framework including verbal and multimodal resources and the emic perspective are the frequently cited strengths of the approach (Heron & Dippold, 2021; Tai, 2021; Pun, 2021). Critics of CA, however, often question its exclusive reliance on the recordings of talk-in-interaction and how that can provide a truly insider perspective (ten Have, 2007). Unless the researchers themselves are part of the community or have a thorough understanding of the local culture, other sources of information might need to be added to the analysis. For example, these other sources are often added by employing an ethnographic approach and might include

Affordances of conversation analysis for investigating EMI 71

Table 5.2 Steps of CA data analysis

Steps	Considerations	Example studies
'Unmotivated look' (ten Have, 2007, pp. 120–121)	Start from the data. What sequences, turns do you notice?	Jacknick and Duran (2021, p. 5) Duran and Sert (2019, p. 76)
Select episodes, sequences to focus on	What are the sequence, turn boundaries? Where does a topic, action start and finish?	Jacknick and Duran (2021, p. 5): IRF with subject-specific concept Duran et al. (2022, p. 507): Word search episodes Duran and Sert (2019, p. 76): Teacher's dispreferred turns-of-action to student responses
Characterise the actions in the sequence	What social action is taking place? What are the participants doing to each other? (e.g. giving instructions, disagreeing, resisting)	Benwell and Stokoe (2002, pp. 433–434): task-setting formulations
Consider the choices of form	What formulations and delivery formats are selected? Would there be other options of forms to be used? What are the interactional consequences of particular forms? What understandings do participants display?	Benwell and Stokoe (2002, pp. 433–434): linguistic features of task-setting sequences Sohn and Spiliotopoulos (2021, p. 94) extracts from conversations according to their functions in the Appendix
Consider aspects of organisation	What is the sequence of the interaction? How is the interaction managed? Turn-taking, sequence organisation, repair organisation	Duran and Sert (2021, p. 7) Jacknick and Duran (2021, pp. 11–12)
Formulate observations	What seem to be general observations and rules of the interaction? What are emerging patterns in terms of turn taking, repair, sequence?	Sohn and Spiliotopoulos (2021, pp. 87–89) Duran et al. (2022, pp. 507–511)
Consider contextual aspects	What kind of norms or features are the participants orienting to?	Duran et al. (2022, pp. 516–517) Chen and Bonacina-Pugh (2021, pp. 118–119)

Based on ten Have (2007, pp. 122–124; Prior & Talmy, 2019; Pomerantz & Fehr, 1997) interviews, stimulated recall interviews with participants, observations and field notes (e.g. Tai, 2021). More recently CA methodology has also been combined with quantitative approaches, such as corpus linguistics. O'Keeffe and Walsh (2012) argue that this combined approach helps investigate the relationship between interaction patterns and linguistic choices and consider whether and how learning opportunities are created or prevented.

Drawing on the affordances of a CA methodology as demonstrated in this chapter, future EMI research could benefit from such CA studies especially by focusing on the following aspects of EMI:

- Interactional dynamics of EMI classroom talk: interaction for learning, scaffolding, equity and social inclusion, knowledge co-construction, display of knowledge and understanding.
- Multiple languages in interaction: construction of implicit or explicit language policy, interaction patterns of language-related episodes, code-switching and translanguaging.
- Multimodal resources in EMI classroom talk: laughter, silence, visual resources, especially as these might be displayed and perceived culturally differently.
- Small-group student interaction: integration of students from diverse backgrounds, 'off-topic' episodes.

Overall, the fact that the present overview had to primarily draw on studies conducted in contexts other than EMI (language teaching, CLIL, school and Anglophone higher education contexts) reminds us of the scarcity of CA studies in EMI research. The nuanced understanding of classroom talk that a CA approach enables has great potential to inform stakeholders and policymakers about effective practices and use of talk for learning in EMI classrooms. Professional development and initial teacher training could also draw on a better understanding, CA studies can provide, of the interactional dynamics in these multilingual and multicultural educational contexts. Future EMI research, therefore, should better harness the affordances of a CA approach.

References

Arkoudis, S., Watty, K., Baik, C., et al. (2013). Finding common ground: Enhancing interaction between domestic and international students in higher education. *Teaching in Higher Education*, *18*(3), 222–235.

Benwell, B. M., & Stokoe, E. H. (2002). Constructing discussion tasks in university tutorials: Shifting dynamics and identities. *Discourse Studies*, *4*(4), 429–453.

Chaudron, C. (1982). Vocabulary elaboration in teachers' speech to L2 *learners. Studies in Second Language Acquisition*, *4*(2), 170–180.

Chen, Q., & Bonacina-Pugh, F. (2021). Spotlights on "practiced" language policy in the internationalised university. In M. Heron & D. Dippold (Eds.), *Meaningful teaching interaction at the internationalised university* (pp. 25–38). Routledge.

Curle, S., Jablonkai, R. R., Mittelmeier, J., Sahan, K., & Veitch, A. (2020). English medium part 1: Literature review. In N. Galloway (Ed.), *English in higher education* (Report No. 978-0-86355-977-8). British Council.

Dalton-Puffer, C. (2007). *Discourse in content and language integrated learning (CLIL) classrooms*. John Benjamins.

Dang, T., & Vu, T. (2020). English-medium instruction in the Australian higher education: Untold stories of academics from non-native English-speaking backgrounds. *Current Issues in Language Planning, 21*(3), 279–300.

Duran, D., Kurhila, S., & Sert, O. (2022). Word search sequences in teacher-student interaction in an English as medium of instruction context. *International Journal of Bilingual Education and Bilingualism, 25*(2), 502–521. http://doi.org/10.1080/13670050.2019.1703896

Duran, D., & Sert, O. (2019). Preference organisation in English Medium of instruction classrooms in Turkey higher education setting. *Linguistics and Education, 49*, 72–85.

Duran, D. & Sert, O. (2021). Student-initiated multi-unit questions in EMI classrooms. *Linguistics and Education, 65*, 100980 https://doi.org/10.1016/j.linged.2021.100980

ELAN (Version 6.4) [Computer software]. (2022). *Nijmegen: Max Planck institute for psycholinguistics, the language archive*. https://archive.mpi.nl/tla/elan

Flowerdew, J. (1992). Definitions in science lectures. *Applied Linguistics, 13*(2), 202–221.

Goffman, E. (1967). *Interaction ritual: essays on face-to-face interaction*. Aldine.

Goffman, E. (1974). *Frame analysis: An essay on the organisation of experience*. New York: Harper & Row.

Goffman, E. (1981). *Forms of talk*. Philadelphia, PA: University of Pennsylvania Press.

Green, C., & Lambert, J. (2019). Position vectors, homologous chromosomes and gamma rays: Promoting disciplinary literacy through Secondary Phrase Lists. *English for Specific Purposes, 53*, 1–12.

Hardman, J. (2016). Tutor-student interaction in seminar teaching: Implications for professional development. *Active Learning in Higher Education, 17*(1), 63–76. https://doi.org/10.1177/1469787415616728

Hardman, J. (2021). Pedagogical renewal: Promoting a dialogic pedagogy in the internationalised 21st-century higher education. In M. Heron & D. Dippold (Eds.), *Meaningful teaching interaction at the internationalised university* (pp. 25–38). Routledge.

Heller, V. (2016). Meanings at hand: Coordinating semiotic resources in explaining mathematical terms in classroom discourse. *Classroom Discourse, 7*(3), 253–275.

Heron, M., & Dippold, D. (2021). *Meaningful teaching interaction at the internationalised university*. Routledge.

Jacknick, C. M., & Duran, D. (2021). Transforming student contributions into subject-specific expression. *System, 98*, 102485. https://doi.org/10.1016/j.system.2021.102485

Jefferson, G. (2004). Glossary of transcript symbols with an introduction. In G. H. Lerner (Ed.), *Conversation analysis: Studies from the first generation* (pp. 13–31.). John Benjamins.

Jenks, C. (2021). *Researching classroom discourse: a student guide*. Routledge.

Koole, T. (2010). Displays of epistemic access: Student responses to teacher explanations. *Research on Language and Social Interaction, 43*(2), 183–209.

Lazaraton, A. (2004). Gestures and speech in the vocabulary explanation of one ESL teacher: A microanalytic inquiry. *Language Learning, 54*(1), 79–117.

Llinares, A., & Morton, T. (2010). Historical explanations as situated practice in content and language integrated learning. *Classroom Discourse, 1*(1), 65–84.

Macaro, E., Tian, L., & Chu, L. (2018). First and second language use in English medium instruction contexts. *Language Teaching Research*, 1–21.

Malström, H., Mezek, S., Pecorari, D., Shaw, P., & Irvine, A. (2017). Engaging with terminology in the multilingual classroom: Teachers' practices for bridging the gap between L1 lectures and English reading. *Classroom Discourse*, 8, 3–18.

Markee, N. (1995). Teachers' answers to students' questions: Problematizing the issue of making meaning. *Issues in Applied Linguistics*, 6(2), 63–92.

Markee, N. (2005). Conversation analysis for second language acquisition. In E. Hinkel (Ed.), *Handbook of research in second language teaching and learning* (pp. 344–374). Lawrence Erlbaum.

Mazak, C. M., & Herbas-Donoso, C. (2015). Translanguaging practices at a bilingual university: A case study of a science classroom. *International Journal of Bilingual Education and Bilingualism*, 18(6), 698–714.

Mehan, H. (1979). *Learning lessons: Social organization in the classroom*. Harvard University Press.

Mercer, N. (2000). *Words and minds*. Routledge.

Mortensen, K. (2011). Doing word explanation in interaction. In G. Pallotti & J. Wagner (Eds.), *L2 learning as social practice: Conversation-analytic perspectives* (pp. 135–163). National Foreign Language Resource Center.

Morton, T. (2015). Vocabulary explanations in CLIL classrooms: A conversation analysis perspective. *Language Learning Journal*, 43(3), 256–270.

O'Keeffe, A., & Walsh, S. (2012). Applying corpus linguistics and conversation analysis in the investigation of small group teaching in higher education. *Corpus Linguistics and Linguistics Theory*, 8(1), 159–181.

Pomerantz, A. M., & Fehr, B. J. (1997). Conversation analysis: An approach to the study of social action as sense making practices. In T. A. van Dijk (Ed.), *Discourse as social interaction* (pp. 64–91). Sage.

Prior, M. T., & Talmy, S. (2019). A discursive psychological approach to the analysis of talk and text in applied linguistics. In J. McKinley & H. Rose (Eds.), *Routledge handbook of research methods in applied linguistics*. Routledge.

Pun, J. (2021). Research conducted on classroom interaction in the English medium instruction context. In J. Pun & S. Curle (Eds.), *Research methods in EMI* (pp. 16–31) Routledge.

Rapley, T. (2008). *Doing conversation, discourse and document analysis*. Sage.

Richard, K. & Seedhouse, P. (Eds.). (2005). *Applying conversation analysis*. Palgrave Macmillan.

Sacks, H., Schegloff, E. A., & Jefferson, G. (1974). A simplest systematics for the organization of turntaking for conversation. *Language*, 50(4), 696–735.

Schegloff, E., Jefferson, G., & Sacks, H. (1977). The preference for self-correction in the organization of repair in conversation. *Language*, 53(2), 361–382.

Seedhouse, P. (2004). *The interactional architecture of the language classroom: A conversation analysis perspective*. Blackwell.

Seedhouse, P., Walsh, S., & Jenks, C. (Eds.). (2010). *Conceptualising 'learning' in applied linguistics*. Palgrave Macmillan.

Silverman, D. (Ed.). (2016). *Qualitative research*. Sage.

Sinclair, J. M., & Coulthard, R. M. (1975). *Towards an analysis of discourse: The English used by teachers and pupils*. London: Oxford University Press.

Sohn, B., & Spiliotopoulos, V. (2021). Scaffolding peer interaction within a language- and- content integrated business curriculum: A case study in a western Canadian university. In M. Heron & D. Dippold (Eds.), *Meaningful teaching interaction at the internationalised university* (pp. 80–96). Routledge.

Stokoe, E. H. (2000). Constructing topicality in university students' small-group discussion: A conversation analytic approach. *Language & Education, 14*(3), 184–203.

Tai, K. W. H. (2021). Researching translanguaging in EMI classrooms. In J. Pun & S. Curle (Eds.), *Research methods in EMI* (pp. 120–132). Routledge.

ten Have, P. (2007). *Doing conversation analysis* (2nd ed.). Sage.

Thornbury, S., & Slade, D. (2006). *Conversation: From description to pedagogy*. Cambridge University Press.

Vygotsky, L. S. (1978). *Mind in society: The development of higher psychological processes*. Harvard University Press.

Walsh, S. (2011). *Exploring classroom discourse: Language in action*. London and New York: Routledge.

Wang, W., & Curdt-Christiansen, X. L. (2019). Translanguaging in a Chinese—English bilingual education programme: A university-classroom ethnography. *International Journal of Bilingual Education and Bilingualism, 22*(3), 322–337. http://doi.org/10.1080/13670050.2018.1526254

Waring, H. Z., Creider, C. C., & Box, C. D. (2013). Explaining vocabulary in the second language classroom: A conversation analytic account. *Learning, Culture, and Social Interaction, 2*(4), 249–264.

Webb, N. M., Franke, M. L., De, T., Chan, A. G., Freund, D., Shein, P., & Melkonian, D. K. (2009). 'Explain to your partner': Teachers' instructional practices and students' dialogue in small groups. *Cambridge Journal of Education, 39*(1), 49–70.

Wilkinson, S. (1998). Study abroad from the participants' perspective: A challenge to common beliefs. *Foreign Language Annals, 31*(1), 23–39.

Wong, J., & Waring, H. Z. (2010). *Conversation analysis and second language pedagogy: A guide for ESL/EFL teachers*. Routledge.

6 Moving beyond language in EMI research

A multimodal and multichannel analytical framework to visualise classroom practices

Balbina Moncada-Comas and Irati Diert-Boté

6.1 Project overview and context

In this chapter, we would like to delve into a methodology that we have been employing recently in order to explore English-medium instruction (EMI) classroom practices from a qualitative perspective. This methodological framework encompasses the combination of classroom observation of audio-/video-recorded sessions and ethnographic knowledge obtained through interviews with the lecturer and classroom materials from the subject. In the following pages, we will unravel how we implement this method in order to obtain a detailed and comprehensive picture of the reality of the EMI classroom by focusing on an episode of an EMI lecturer within the field of Tourism.

In the beginning, our paths analysing classroom practices (EMI and English for Specific Purposes, ESP) utilised a combination of Membership Categorisation Analysis and Positioning Theory (Moncada-Comas & Block, 2019), small stories and Narrative Positioning (Diert-Boté & Martin-Rubió, 2018). However, we felt that something was missing, as the approaches chosen as well as the data analysed only focused on speech and interaction without any emphasis on *action*. Therefore, our methodological tools experienced a 'multimodal turn' and subsequently we started to flirt with the combination of various modes in order to fully approach the whole teaching and learning process. These methodological advances have been made possible thanks to the so-called 'video turn' (Mondada, 2019), which allows the researchers to obtain repeated observations of the detailed actions that occurred in situ involving —in this case— key EMI stakeholders (i.e. lecturer and students). This method derived from conversation analysis, so it is relatively new inasmuch as it uses video recordings, although it has been gaining increased attention lately in different contexts including EMI (Morell et al., 2008; Morell et al., 2022; Morell et al., 2020).

DOI: 10.4324/9781003375531-7

First, Diert-Boté published two articles integrating self-reported and classroom data, the latter analysed multimodally but mostly focusing on the verbal aspects of the teacher–student interaction (see Diert-Boté, 2023, in press). Second, Moncada-Comas started paying attention to students' interaction and realised how different modes played an important role in the communicative process (Moncada-Comas, 2021). Following the same method, the spotlight then turned on the teacher by investigating how lecturers' multimodal competence facilitated the learning experience (Moncada-Comas & Sabaté-Dalmau, in press). These two publications drew on Morell's (2018) multimodal discourse analysis, which provides a sound instrument to explore multimodally classroom data:

> The multimodal perspective takes into account *how* the instructors carry out the lesson by referring to the linguistic and paralinguistic affordances of speech and writing, the potential of their use of non-verbal materials and body language, as well as their orchestration of modes.
> (Morell, 2018, p. 72, emphasis in original)

Our paths eventually met in a joint publication in which we analysed an ESP lecturer not only by adopting a multimodal perspective, but also by adding to the analysis a multichannel angle (Moncada-Comas & Diert-Boté, 2022), thus achieving an even more integrative analytical framework. With this approach, apart from the multiple semiotic modes, we also analyse the various channels of communication employed in the classroom contexts (mostly technological learning channels) through which students' disciplinary literacies are also developed. The aforementioned study enabled us to examine both online and onsite classroom practices, as incorporating multichannel analysis contributed significantly to our understanding of the use of technology in class. Accordingly, we became aware that the use of technology in class is here to stay, as it can contribute and promote the acquisition of language and content and, thus, it is worth looking further into it.

Overall, we are interested in the study of EMI classroom practices through the integration of a multimodal and a multichannel framework because it provides a more holistic view of how meaning is conveyed and how linguistic, paralinguistic and non-linguistic features interplay in the classroom setting. Particularly, we are driven to this methodology because content and language knowledge construction occurs not only through speech, but also through the ensemble of resources that facilitate the understanding of verbal language.

6.2 Research planning

Our research stems from the LIDISELF project (*Development of disciplinary literacies in English as a lingua franca at university*), which departed from the reality that the internationalisation of Higher Education (HE) institutions has brought about the implementation of EMI. The aim of this project is to inquire into the students' development of disciplinary literacies through academic genres across EMI, ESP and L1 subjects. In order to investigate the acquisition of disciplinary literacies, a mixed-methods approach was applied by collecting data from questionnaires, interviews and classroom observation and assessed students' written and oral productions.

As the project aimed at comparing STEM (Science, Technology, Engineering and Mathematics) and SSCC (Social Sciences) courses, our research focused on the latter and, particularly, we have examined Business, Tourism, and Audiovisual Communication and Journalism EMI and ESP courses. In this chapter, we specifically focus on the field of Tourism for which a total of six classes were part of the corpus: two L1 subjects, two EMI subjects and two ESP subjects. At the moment, we are comparing ESP and EMI teachers' multimodal competence, and multilingual and multichannel awareness to identify similarities and differences in their teaching practices (see Sabaté-Dalmau & Moncada-Comas, in press, for a holistic integration of a multimodal, multichannel and plurilingual approach in EMI).

On the whole, the major novelty of the LIDISELF project lies in the specific focus on how lecturers help develop students' disciplinary literacies through specific genres of their field by zooming into how lecturers teach specific academic and professional genres. Our particular contribution is to continue advancing in the knowledge of how teacher–student (inter)action makes visible the different multimodal and multichannel resources that result in (in)effective teaching practices. Therefore, in this chapter we will illustrate how the multimodal and multichannel analytical framework can be employed in order to analyse an EMI lecturer in action in the classroom setting.

6.3 Research design

Taking into account the research project background and objectives, this study follows a qualitative research design in an attempt to approach EMI classroom practices in real action and observe the teaching strategies that are employed to facilitate meaning-making and to build disciplinary knowledge. In order to understand the differences between qualitative and quantitative research methods, Croker (2009) contrasts constructivism and positivism, two of the most well-known paradigms that are frequently used as examples of opposing viewpoints. On the one hand, positivists search for a single, all-encompassing 'truth' arguing that there is an unchanging reality that has to be described, typically by quantification. On the other hand, constructivists believe that there is no universal 'truth' and that each person builds their own reality, which 'is not only universal but person-, context-, and time-bound' (Croker, 2009, p. 6).

In this study, the classroom is viewed as an ecology (van Lier, 2004) or a complex dynamic system (Larsen-Freeman & Cameron, 2008) in which learning is regarded as a process that develops through the interaction of all of its components/agents, and the interactions between the people at all levels: cognitive, emotional, behavioural, social and discursive. It is precisely this interaction with their environment that enables individuals to socially construct meaning. Therefore, questions such as 'What's going on here? What does the world look like for participants? What meanings do they make here? How does this setting influence participants' perceptions and behavior?' (Croker, 2009, p. 8) become significant to comprehend the participants' subjective meanings. Due to the complexity of the conceptualisation and the nature of the research questions, it is assumed that a constructionist, qualitative, interpretative method is required to thoroughly examine the teachers' experiences and practices on an individual and a societal level.

Within qualitative research, ethnography allows the researchers to have a 'prolonged engagement within a specific community' (Starfield, 2010, p. 51) that is 'based on direct observation' (Gobo, 2011, p. 15). Therefore, the ethnographic method does not involve an experimental context, but participants are observed in their everyday practices —in this case EMI practices. As the researcher becomes the primary instrument to collect and analyse data, a variety of research procedures and instruments are employed to avoid biases and guarantee trustworthiness. These data collection methods are observational and non-observational (Burns, 2009): observational methods in classroom research include field notes, audio- or video-recordings of the class, observation of the classroom activities, maps/layouts of the classroom and photographs of the physical context. On the other hand, non-observational methods encompass questionnaires and surveys, interviews, class discussions or focus groups, diaries, journals and logs, and classroom documents (materials used, sample activities or tests). All the specifications in terms of data collection methods and analysis will be elaborated further in the next section.

6.4 Methods

6.4.1 Data collection

Data were collected from the EMI course *Quality Management in Tourism*, which is an optional subject taught to four-year students at the University of Lleida (UdL). In our research, data triangulation allows for the acquisition of information at various levels and from different techniques or data sets, resulting in a more reliable study (Flick, 2018). More specifically, we draw on the following non-observational and observational tools and procedures:

(a) classroom observation and audio/video-recordings with one video camera pointing at lecturer's action, observing a total of four classes during the course; (b) semi-structured pre- and post-interviews to ensure a prolonged engagement with participants; and (c) collection of classroom materials and resources. The core data set is classroom interaction obtained through video-recorded data. Nevertheless, to complement the analysis of classroom practices, the other sets (b and c) have been considered in order to build the authors' ethnographic knowledge to help develop a comprehensive picture of the EMI reality.

6.4.1.1 Classroom observation and audio–video recording

Classroom observation (and audio/video recordings) was the central data collection procedure, as it provides real-life information (Dörnyei, 2007). Gaudet and Robert (2018) point out that '[t]he idea behind observation is to get as close as possible to, if not actually into, the reality you are studying' (p. 80). In order to obtain a direct window to the classroom ecology, the use of video cameras in qualitative social research has become the 'data collection tool of choice' to explore situated interactions in natural settings like classrooms (Jewitt, 2012, p. 2). Thus, video recordings are a rich information source, which can be watched as many times as needed in order to spot interesting extracts which can be later transcribed. Regarding transcription, Coates and Thornborrow (1999) argue that there is no perfect transcript, as this will always be a partial representation of reality based on the goal of the research; however, this is not seen as a drawback but as a necessity.

Four lessons were observed with a camera directed to the EMI lecturer to capture her speech and actions. Researchers did not interfere during classroom observation but rather observed and collected facts with a minimum impact in order to gather an exhaustive amount of data about what occurs in the educational context analysed, for example, teaching strategies employed, and multilingual, multimodal and multichannel practices present in the class. Once the observations were completed, the video and audio recordings were then stored securely in the project database.

One limitation regarding classroom data collection is the fact that the lecturer was not fitted with a wireless recorder connected to a lapel microphone, which can sometimes hamper the understanding of her speech. Moreover, it has to be mentioned that we did not record students' practices or conversations (student–student interactions) and no camera was directed to the student cohort; hence, only the lecturer's voice and actions are clearly heard and seen. Although student–student interactions may be as valuable, the focus needs to be narrow and precise to guarantee a sound micro multimodal and multichannel analysis of meaning conveyance. If student–student or teacher–student interactions are the focus of the study, it is necessary to distribute various recorders on students' desks to capture their contributions. Similarly, in this case we also recommend taking field notes and mapping the layout of the classroom to record the positioning of the students in the class.

6.4.1.2 Pre- and post- semi-structured interviews

Interviews have been depicted as 'the gold standard of qualitative research' (Silverman, 2000, p. 51), as they provide valuable insights into participants' experiences, perceptions and beliefs (among others) in a way that is not possible with questionnaires (Richards, 2009). In semi-structured interviews, the researcher usually follows a guide with the key pre-set topics or questions while allowing a degree of flexibility 'to elaborate on the issues raised in an explanatory manner' (Dörnyei, 2011, p. 136). These semi-structured interviews offered informants the opportunity to expand on the *why*, *how* and *what for* of their practices, experiences and expectations about teaching in an EMI context.

On the one hand, pre-interviews (carried out at the beginning of the course) were designed in order (1) to explore lecturers' linguistic and academic backgrounds and trajectories, (2) to look into their teaching experience, (3) to identify the types of academic genres they teach, and (4) to examine the role of English and other languages in class. On the other hand, post-interviews (after course completion) were carried out (1) to gather impressions about the subject, (2) to provide more details about activity instructions and assessment instruments, (3) to delve into the types of genres that are produced on each task, and (4) to reflect upon the language policy implemented in the classroom.

One important limitation in the design of these interview guides is the fact that no multimodal/multichannel questions were posed as this was not the main objective of the research project, but a research area deemed appropriate after classroom observation. Nevertheless, this was counterbalanced in the post-interview script by adding specific questions that deal with the lecturer's use of multimodal and multichannel practices (see Appendix 1). Despite this, it is worth mentioning that, bearing in mind the specificity of the topics, some informants may not give as much detail about them as others, and some issues may be tackled only superficially, as was the case in our data set. In addition, it is interesting to note that interviews were conducted both face-to-face (F2F) and online due to the COVID-19 pandemic. This may be seen as a drawback given that conversation flows more smoothly in an onsite environment as, in a virtual setting, technical issues (e.g. internet connection or background noises, among others) may arise.

6.4.1.3 Collection of classroom materials and others

The last set of data involved the collection of classroom materials and resources as peripheral information to build contextual and ethnographic knowledge for the authors. Among this collection, we can find consent forms, the subject teaching guide, PowerPoint presentations, dossiers, tasks' instructions and rubrics, students' oral and written submissions and examinations and teacher's communication with students (e-mails), among others.

6.4.2 *Data analysis*

In relation to data analysis, a multimodal and multichannel analysis has been employed. This method allows us to approach the interactional episode with greater detail taking into account the whole orchestration of modes and channels involved. Multimodality questions the predominance of linguistic models, embracing other meaning-making resources, such as images, gestures and movements. Multimodal phenomena (i.e., the interaction between different semiotic modes) may guarantee 'semantic expansion' (O'Halloran, 2018), that is, the potential to expand semantic associations by integrating different resources in the meaning-making process. Finally, multichannel analysis is related to the *medium*, 'the materiality of the multimodal artefact, including the technology or other medium involved (e.g., book, interactive digital media)' (O'Halloran, 2018, p. 125). The objective, and challenge, of combining multimodal and multichannel analysis is to gather as much detail as possible about the complexity of interactional episodes that occur in the EMI classroom setting.

One of the major dilemmas regarding this research is data reporting due to the need to abide by data protection constraints (ensuring the anonymity of informants) while keeping our commitment to micro-multimodal-multichannel analysis. In order to preserve our informant's anonymity, we have blurred her face or any other information that may reveal her identity. In order to report the data in as much detail as possible, episodes were divided into three teaching moves (i.e., pedagogical functions), that were then further categorised into meaningful units (dynamic spatial positions, DSPs). All these small meaningful units were then transcribed verbatim including as many details as possible (i.e., paralinguistic features of language such as stress and pauses) (see Appendix 2 for Transcription Conventions). In addition, whenever possible screenshots were taken to provide an account of the gestures, moves or positioning of the lecturer (i.e., video stills that show gestures, movements around the classroom and proxemics in relation to students). One last aspect that was considered when reporting data is the need to refer to the complementary teaching materials and mediums used (i.e. channels such as technology) that complement the meaning-making process. Finally, a commentary column was needed to clarify certain multimodal and multichannel aspects (see Appendix 3 for the Table Template).

One of the downsides of using this method is that it involves a micro-level analysis that requires as much precision as possible. For this reason, we recommend focusing on a meaningful and relevant episode to inquire into a specific teaching or learning practice. By way of illustration, in Moncada-Comas and Diert-Boté (2022), the extract lasted less than 10 minutes, but the transcription added up to 1,526 words and occupied eight pages. Another limitation, going back to Coates and Thornborow's (1999) idea, is that all transcripts are in a way biased even though they try to capture reality as objectively as possible. From our experience, we realised that when including the comments about multimodal and multichannel aspects, we were already pre-analysing the data (e.g. attempting to describe gestures and facial expressions); however, these interpretations are endorsed by the fact that researchers and the informant share the same sociocultural background. Finally, the last shortcoming is that only researchers have access to the complete video-recording of the excerpt, and readers have a limited access to it through the selected stills chosen by the researchers (which again may increase subjectivity).

6.5 An example of the methodology in use

In this section we provide the readers with an example of how this micro-level analytical framework is put into practice, thus shedding some light on its practical applications and contributions to EMI research.

As we have been mentioning throughout the chapter, the multimodal and multichannel framework is particularly useful to analyse in-depth classroom observation data, including those from EMI settings, from a micro perspective. Therefore, we will implement this methodology with an example that illustrates the analytical procedure taken from a single case study with a female EMI lecturer (Jana, pseudonym) in the Tourism bachelor's degree. It is important to note here that this lecturer did not have any experience teaching at a higher education nor teaching in English (EMI); hence, this was her first time performing the role of *EMI lecturer*. Her English language certified competence is a B2 according to the Common European Framework of Reference for Languages (CEFR), but in her bachelor's degree in Business studies, half of the subjects were taught in English, hence she was familiar with EMI as a student. Despite her linguistic background, there was no actual requirement for this position. In fact, she was offered the opportunity to teach this subject in English and she accepted due to her positive view of internationalisation and Englishisation in Higher Education institutions (see Diert-Boté & Moncada-Comas, 2023 for more details about Jana's professional identity and self-concept).

Lessons were divided into a first theoretical part followed by a more practical section. A total of four class sessions were recorded: three both audio- and video-recorded (two onsite and one online) and one only audio-recorded.

These classes were recorded throughout the semester to collect longitudinal data: one in September, two in October and the last one in December. Overall, there are 4 hours and 15 minutes of footage. For this analysis, we will present data from one of the sessions that was audio-/video-recorded (14 September 2021) in order to gather both verbal and non-verbal data. In this lesson, we have identified three teaching moves: (1) the introduction move (0:00–20:11); (2) the presentation of key notions move (20:12–30:05); and (3) the explanation of the teaching guide move (30:06–47:42). The data analysed in this chapter (see Appendix 4) come from a specific episode from *move 2*, during which the teacher encouraged students to discuss different topics related to the subject of quality management in tourism.

In this episode of nearly 2 minutes (1'40''), we can observe how orchestration of multimodal and multichannel ensembles comes into play. First of all, DSP 1 shows that the lecturer gazes at students' faces to check for understanding. Thanks to her multimodal awareness, she notices that one student needs further clarification and so she provides the Spanish term ('*PIB*') for the English equivalent ('GDP'). In DSP 2, the teacher uses the classroom space as she moves closer to the projected screen and even touches the screen to refer to specific contents. We can observe the lecturer employing a lot of hand gestures in DSP 3. A common gesture that accompanies Jana's speech is the so-called baton (beat) gesture. This type of gesture emphasises particular aspects of speech, 'ha[s] only two movement phases, for example up and down' (Alibali et al., 2001, p. 175), and provides no semantic meaning. In addition, the lecturer also employs deictic gestures, which 'nicely map onto deictic expressions like "this" and "that," "these" and "those," "here" and "there"' (Louwerse & Bangerter, 2005, p. 1332). These are used when she wants to direct the students' attention towards a specific point in the projected screen ('these data') and when she wants to highlight a specific point in time ('right now'). Moreover, metaphorical or symbolic gestures are also common as they 'represent directly a specific object or action (e.g. nodding the head, waving "goodbye"), based on conventionality or habit within the same cultural group' (Cochet & Vauclair, 2014, p. 280). These movements are used when Jana represents with her hands the verbs 'to split up' and 'to spend money', or when she wants to represent an approximate number ('it's like the si- the six percent of the total amount of money').

In the extract analysed, there are not many channels involved other than face-to-face communication and the use of a PowerPoint presentation, which is quite visually attractive. In fact, in the pre-interview, Jana mentioned: 'my slides were very visual . . . for example a text-based slide was split into two separate slides adding a lot of pictures and examples' (Jana's pre-interview, 21 September 2021). It has to be mentioned that the lecturer also employs other technological tools at the end of the lesson when she plays a video to provide students with a sample of quality in tourism (this extract has not been added due to space constraints). Indeed, the introduction of technological tools is transforming traditional educational environments to make the most of digital resources and thus providing students with more resources than those offered in the typical lecture (Querol-Julián & Crawford Camiciottoli, 2019). Nevertheless, the data analysed show that her multichannel practices are limited in relation to students' class engagement, as they are not fully involved in the lesson and barely participate. For example, it remains unclear how the video can assist in the students' learning process, as there is no activity (e.g. reflection or discussion) to perform after watching it. Therefore, the inclusion of technology in class does not necessarily imply that the teaching-learning process is successful, or even more enjoyable or motivating for students, as it appears to be the case here. For this reason, the use of technology in class has to be pedagogically justified and a clear objective needs to be set to ensure effective instruction (Moncada-Comas & Diert-Boté, 2022).

As it can be observed from the classroom excerpt analysed, a multimodal and multichannel methodology allows us to identify both effective and ineffective teaching practices by taking heed of the aggregation of (1) the languages used (English and others) through the verbal transcription; (2) the paralinguistic and non-linguistic aspects of the teaching-learning process through the detailed transcript, the video stills and the commentary box; and (3) the technological tools employed thanks to the channels column. This analysis also opens a new opportunity to identify the shortcomings and strengths of EMI teaching practices in order to implement relevant training programmes for EMI lecturers. Finally, the fact that classroom data are accompanied with interview data encourages lecturers' self-reflection on their practices and the extent to which they implement multilingual, multimodal and multichannel strategies.

6.6 Conclusion

This chapter has focused on how a micro-level qualitative methodology such as multimodal and multichannel analysis can be used to strengthen EMI research. This method can be useful to analyse data from a different but accurate lens, as it helps to consider the whole picture of the EMI classroom. Bearing this in mind, our research implements a holistic and solid micro analysis of EMI practice in action, taking into consideration all teaching resources: languages, modes and channels. This research methodology points out that knowledge transmission and construction do not rely solely on the use of language; in contrast, many other elements that lecturers employ are essential to facilitating and making more accessible the disciplinary contents being taught. This type of analysis ensures that all meaning-making resources employed by EMI lecturers are considered when analysing EMI teaching practices, as all of them add up to the learning process. Therefore, and more specifically, this framework has been useful to identify how the teacher can combine and make use of different elements for various pedagogical purposes. For example, multimodal resources include a variety of gestures to accompany speech and explanations; proxemics and positioning demonstrate that the use of different spaces in the class may express closeness to students; and paralinguistic features (stress, volume, tone) are shown to be useful to highlight certain information. Finally, this analytical framework enables us to spot multichannel resources with the use of various technological tools that can be used efficiently, provided that they have a pedagogical purpose.

Acknowledgements

This research has been carried out thanks to the grant LIDISELF-PID2019-107451GB-I00/AEI/10.13039/501100011033 from the Spanish Ministry of Economy and Competitiveness and 2021 SGR 01295 from Generalitat de Catalunya . The authors are indebted to the lecturer who participated in the study.

References

Alibali, M. W., Heath, D. C., & Myers, H. J. (2001). Effects of visibility between speaker and listener on gesture production: Some gestures are meant to be seen. *Journal of Memory and Language, 44*(2), 169–188. https://doi.org/10.1006/jmla.2000.2752

Burns, A. (2009). Action research. In J. Heigham & R. A. Croker (Eds.), *Qualitative research in applied linguistics: A practical introduction* (pp. 112–134). Palgrave Macmillan.

Coates, J., & Thornborrow, J. (1999). Myths, lies and audiotapes: Some thoughts on data transcripts. *Discourse and Society, 10*(4), 594–597.

Cochet, H., & Vauclair, J. (2014). Deictic gestures and symbolic gestures produced by adults in an experimental context: Hand shapes and hand preferences. *Laterality: Asymmetries of Body, Brain and Cognition, 19*(3), 278–301. https://doi.org/10.1080/1357650X.2013.804079.

Croker, R. (2009). An introduction to qualitative research. In J. Heigham & R. Croker (Eds.), *Qualitative research in applied linguistics: A practical introduction* (pp. 3–24). Palgrave Macmillan.

Diert-Boté, I. (2023). Positivity in the English language learning classroom: An analysis of teacher-student moments of contact. *Revista Española de Lingüística Aplicada. (36)* 2, 1-29. https://doi.org/10.1075/resla.20057.die

Diert-Boté, I. (in press). The dynamics of an EFL learner's speaking self-concept: Insights from self-reported accounts and classroom observation data. *Revista Brasileira de Linguistica Aplicada.*

Diert-Boté, I., & Martin-Rubió, M. (2018). Learning English in catalonia: Beliefs and emotions through small stories and iterativity. *Narrative Inquiry, 28*(1), 56–74. https://doi.org/10.1075/ni.17029.die

Diert-Boté, I., & Moncada-Comas, B. (2023). Analyzing EMI Lecturer Perceptions About the Self: Insights Into Their Professional Identities and Self-Concepts. In S. Karpava (Ed.), *Handbook of Research on Language Teacher Identity* (pp. 131–153). IGI Global. https://doi.org/10.4018/978-1-6684-7275-0.ch008

Dörnyei, Z. (2007). *Research methods in applied linguistics: Quantitative, qualitative and mixed methodologies*. Oxford University Press.

Dörnyei, Z. (2011). *Research methods in applied linguistics*. University Press.

Flick, U. (2018). Triangulation in data collection. In U. Flick (Ed.), *The SAGE handbook of qualitative data collection* (pp. 527–544). Sage.

Gaudet, S., & Robert, D. (2018). *A journey through qualitative research. From design to reporting*. Sage.

Gobo, G. (2011) Ethnography. In D. Silverman (Ed.), *Qualitative research* (3rd ed., pp. 15–36). Sage.

Jewitt, C. (2012). An introduction to using video for research (Unpublished paper). *National Centre for Research Methods*. http://eprints.ncrm.ac.uk/2259/

Larsen-Freeman, D., & Cameron, L. (2008). *Complex systems and applied linguistics*. Oxford University Press.

Louwerse, M. M., & Bangerter, A. (2005). Focusing attention with deictic gestures and linguistic expressions. *Proceedings of the Annual Meeting of the Cognitive Science Society, 27*, 1331–1336.

Moncada-Comas, B. (2021). "Being a student" and "doing education": A multimodal analysis of backstage and frontstage interactional episodes in EMI. In D. Block & S. Khan (Eds.), *The secret life of English-medium instruction in higher education: Examining microphenomena in context* (pp. 43–69). Routledge.

Moncada-Comas, B., & Block, D. (2019). CLIL-ised EMI in practice: Issues arising. *The Language Learning Journal, 49*(6), 686–698. https://doi.org/10.1080/09571736.2019.1660704

Moncada-Comas, B., & Diert-Boté, I. (2022). Good practices in ESP: The interplay between technology and interaction through multimodal and multichannel practices. In S. García-Sánchez & R. Clouet (Eds.), *Intercultural communication and ubiquitous learning in multimodal English language education* (pp. 146–183). IGI Global. http://doi.org/10.4018/978-1-7998-8852-9.ch008

Moncada-Comas, B., & Sabaté-Dalmau, M. (in press). The role of multimodal competence in "doing EMI lecturing": Exploring the effectiveness of non-linguistic resources in EMI. In V. Beltrán Palanques & E. Bernad Mechó (Eds.), *Integrating content and language in higher education: A multimodal perspective*. Routledge

Mondada, L. (2019). Transcribing silent actions: A multimodal approach of sequence organization. *Social Interaction. Video-based studies of Human Sociality, 2*(1). https://doi.org/10.7146/si.v2i1.113150

Morell, T. (2018). Multimodal competence and effective interactive lecturing. *System, 77*, 70–79. http://doi.org/10.1016/j.system.2017.12.006

Morell, T., Beltrán-Palanques, V., & Norte, N. (2022). A multimodal analysis of pair work engagement episodes: Implications for EMI lecturer training. *Journal of English for Academic Purposes, 58*, 101124. https://doi.org/10.1016/j.jeap.2022.101124

Morell, T., Garcia, M., & Sanchez, I. (2008). Multimodal strategies for effective academic presentation in English for non-native speakers. In R. Monroy & A. Sanchez (Eds.), *25 years of applied linguistics in Spain: Milestones and challenges* (pp. 557–568). Editum.

Morell, T., Norte Fernández-Pacheco, N., & Beltran-Palanques, V. (2020). How do trained English-medium instruction (EMI) lecturers combine multimodal ensembles to engage their students? In R. Roig-Vila (Ed.), *La docencia en la Enseñanza Superior Nuevas aportaciones desde la investigación e innovación educativas* (pp. 308–321). Octaedro.

O'Halloran, K. L. (2018). Multimodal discourse analysis. In K. Hyland & B. Paltgride (Eds.), *The continuum companion to discourse analysis* (pp. 120–137). Continuum.

Querol-Julián, M., & Crawford Camiciottoli, B. (2019). The impact of online technologies and English medium instruction on university lectures in international learning contexts: A systematic review. *ESP Today, 7*(1), 2–23. https://doi.org/10.18485/esptoday.2019.7.1.1

Richards, K. (2009). Interviews. In J. Heigham & R. A. Croker (Eds.) *Qualitative Research in Applied Linguistics: A Practical Introduction* (pp. 182–199). Palgrave Macmillan.

Sabaté-Dalmau, M. & Moncada-Comas, B. (in press). Exploring the Affordances of Multimodal Competence, Multichannel Awareness and Plurilingual Lecturing in EMI. *System*.

Silverman, D. (2000). *Doing Qualitative Research*. Sage Publications.

Starfield, S. (2010). Ethnographies. In B. Paltridge & A. Phakiti (Eds.), *Continuum companion in research methods in applied linguistics* (pp. 50–65). Continuum.

van Lier, L. (2004). *The ecology and semiotics of language learning: A sociocultural perspective*. Kluwer Academic.

Appendices

Appendix 1 Post-interview: Multimodal and multichannel questions

Multimodal

1. Apart from the L1(s), what other resources do you use to facilitate learning and accompany explanations or speech (i.e. non-verbal communication such as gestures or facial communication)?
2. To what extent do you move around the class, shifting from your desk to students' desks? Why and when do you change spaces?
3. To what extent do you emphasise aspects of your speech using tone, volume, stress and even silences or pauses?
4. Are you aware of, students' facial expressions or gestures during the lesson? If you see a student 'confused' or 'sleepy', how do you react? Do you think it is important to pay attention to these non-verbal aspects?
5. Do you think that ESP or EMI classes teachers (as opposed to L1 teachers) should make use of more multimodal resources to engage students as English is a foreign /second language in the subject?

Multichannel

6. Do your teaching practices include the use of technology? If so, what tools do you use?
7. Why do you use ICT tools (e.g. Cloudtagger, YouTube videos, Google or others) in the onsite classroom?
8. In your opinion, to what extent do these digital resources contribute to the teaching-learning process (pedagogical implications)?
9. If you teach online, how do you make sure that students are paying attention? Which tools can contribute to students' engagement and participation?
10. Do you think in ESP or EMI (as opposed to L1 teachers) classes teachers should make use of more multichannel resources to engage students as English is a foreign /second language in the subject?

Appendix 2 Transcription Conventions

Symbol	Function
/	Pauses between speech units
?	Rising intonation
<1>, <2>, <3> ...	Number of gestures, shift of gaze, movement or others (commented in the corresponding column)
</1>, </2>, </3> ...	Closure of gesture, shift of gaze, movement or others (commented in the corresponding column) to mark the duration of the action
:	Lengthened sound (e.g. elongated vowels)
italics	Languages other than English
(1)	Neared number of seconds. For example, (1) = 1 second, (3) = 3 seconds
word_	Unfinished utterance

Appendix 3 Table template for multimodal and multichannel analysis

Time (min='; sec=")	DSP	Verbal speech by the lecturer (and students)	Gestures and movements (stills from video)	Channels	Comments about modes and channels (if necessary)

Moving beyond language in EMI research 91

Appendix 4 Example of data analysis

Time (min=´; sec=´´)	DSP	Verbal speech by the lecturer (and students)	Gestures and movements (stills from video)	Channels	Comments about modes and channels (if necessary)
20´12´´	1	so let's start/em: (4) as you know/ everyones know that is the GDP?/e: the: PIB_/here in Spain/<1> e- el PIB_ e: <2>/here in Spain the GDP_	<1>	F2F + PowerPoint presentation	<1> looks at one student
20´31´´	2	<2> can you see it? <2> <3> you cannot see it S1: no S2: no ok/don't worry/I will explain	<2> <3>	F2F + PowerPoint presentation	<2> & <2> comes closer to the projected screen <3> touches the projected screen

(Continued)

(Continued)

Time (min='; sec=")	DSP	Verbal speech by the lecturer (and students)	Gestures and movements (stills from video)	Channels	Comments about modes and channels (if necessary)
20' 39" 21' 22"	3	here in Spain <4> all the companies that they are doing the projects or the invoice/em tourism is like twelve percent <4> (1)/but <5> these data is from twenty nineteen (1)/so when the covid cames (.) here (.) it's split up <6>/so right now it's not e: twelve/it's like the si- the <7> six percent of the total amount of money that the people are <8> spending <9> right now/here in Spain it's from tourism (.)/so it's a lot of money (.)/so do we have to focus/and also here in Spain (1) there are a lot of sun and a lot of tourists come here to sp- have fun and enjoy	<4> <5> <6>	F2F + PowerPoint presentation	<4> uses baton gestures to emphasise points in her speech <5> uses both hands to point to the screen <6> represents the verb 'split up' with both hands by hitting the right hand against the palm of the left one <7> shakes hand side to side <8> hits left palm with right fist <9> moves hands with both palms downwards

Moving beyond language in EMI research 93

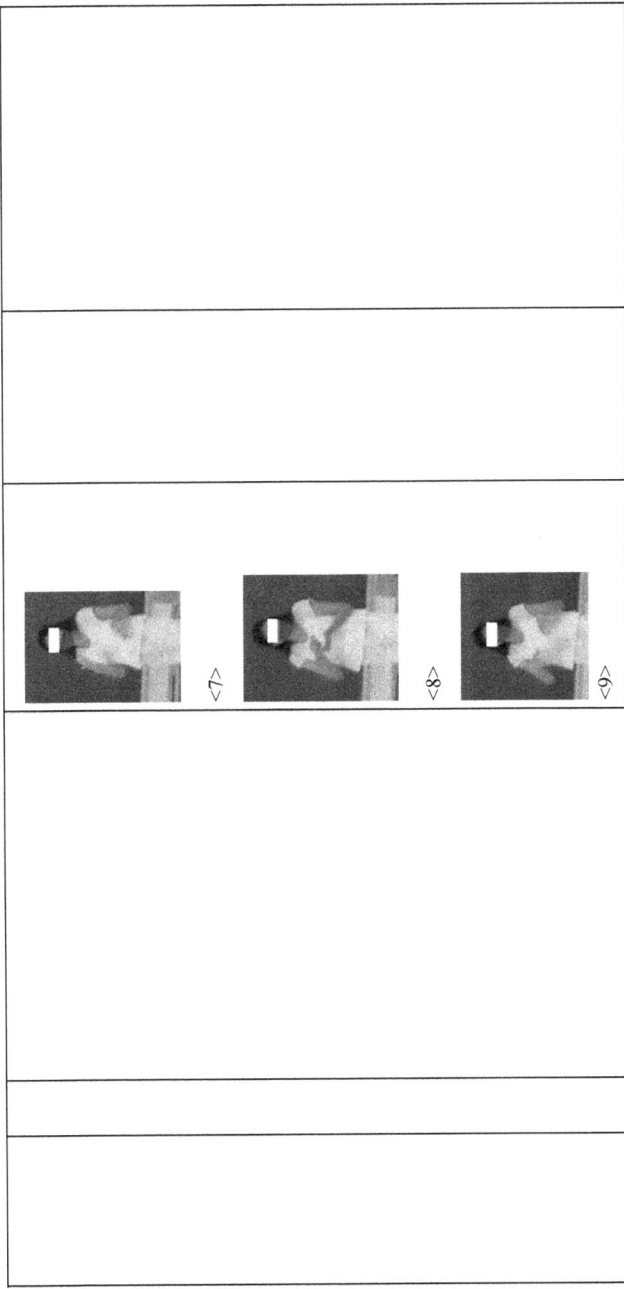

7 A narrative enquiry into EMI instructors' linguistic and pedagogical needs

Sezen Arslan

7.1 Project overview and context

Student mobility has gained momentum thanks to globalisation and the eminent status of English as a lingua franca (Hu & Wu, 2020). Masses of students move to different countries to pursue higher education. There are a quarter-billion students in more than 20,000 universities worldwide (Wit & Altbach, 2021). Attracting international students increases the universities' visibility and global ranking. Therefore, universities strive to expand their opportunities to welcome more international students. This rush for internalisation has then accelerated the shift towards English-medium instruction (EMI) (Galloway & Ruegg, 2020). Content instructors offer courses in English so that students from different countries can understand the content, regardless of their native languages. This is believed to positively impact the students' English proficiency and future careers (Huang & Curle, 2021).

However, EMI at universities brings several issues to the fore regarding the instructors. Among them, the primary concern is whether/to what extent the instructors can teach content in English because they mostly do not receive sufficient and relevant pedagogical training (O'Dowd, 2018). Many of them teach through English in linguistically and culturally diverse settings as a result of the internalisation of the education; therefore, they should not only have a good command of English but also know and use the relevant methodologies to deliver the content in English (Block & Moncada-Comas, 2019). In so doing, they need to be equipped with sufficient proficiency in English, including oral, aural and written abilities and pedagogical skills to teach in English, such as developing materials, designing/evaluating tests and classroom management.

EMI teaching competence centres around some aspects, including linguistics and pedagogy (Fortanet-Gomez, 2020; Gundermann, 2013). For this reason, the EMI teacher training programs must address those components to develop EMI teachers professionally. Therefore, it will be significant to investigate the EMI instructors' linguistic and pedagogical needs.

Investigation and conceptualisation of these needs will inform future EMI teacher training programs. For this purpose, the linguistic and pedagogical needs of EMI instructors in Turkish universities were investigated, and components of an ideal professional development program for EMI instructors were identified based on their perspectives. In so doing, evidence from narrative frames and interview data were used. The reason for using narrative frames in this study is to motivate the instructors to reflect upon their teaching experiences since narrative frames enable guidance for the participants about what to write in terms of structure and content (Barkhuizen & Wette, 2008). Narrative frames help reveal the first-person accounts of teacher experiences (Viet, 2012). Therefore, the participants may understand and interpret their experiences according to the ready-made narratives presented to them (Webster & Mertova, 2007). Narrative frames have been previously used within the EMI context (see Breeze & Roothooft, 2021; Rahman et al., 2022; Roothooft, 2022)

Apart from narrative frames, semi-structured interviews were also used to comprehensively understand the EMI instructors' needs regarding language, instructional implementations, and professional development. Interviews were conducted to obtain more detailed data to describe the participants' thoughts (Geertz, 1973). They were used to ensure the credibility of the interpretations made through narrative frames.

7.2 Research planning

7.2.1 Context of the study

According to constitutional law, the official language of Turkey is Turkish, and no other language can be taught as a native language to Turkish citizens (Legal Gazette, Article 42, 1982). However, English is the only compulsory language taught as a foreign language at all levels of education in Turkey (Kırkgöz, 2009). Given this predominance of English as a foreign language (EFL) in Turkey, in Turkish universities, there are two types of EMI programs which are full and partial EMI. This study focused on EMI instructors that teach in full and partial EMI programs.

7.2.2 Participants

The participants were 37 EMI instructors selected based on their availability within the research context. Throughout this study, pseudonyms were used. All participants were Turkish and spoke English as a foreign language. Three demographic items are of concern: (a) gender, (b) the subjects– Mathematical, Physical and Life Sciences (MPLS) or Social Sciences (Soc) that the instructors taught and c) years of teaching experience as an EMI

Table 7.1 Distribution of participants in terms of demographics

Gender		Subject taught		Years of teaching experience				
Male (%)	Female (%)	MPLS (%)	Soc (%)	0–5 (%)	6–11 (%)	12–17 (%)	18–23 (%)	24 and above (%)
21 (56.8%)	16 (43.2%)	21 56.76%	16 43.24%	10 27.03%	13 35.13%	3 8.11%	7 18.92%	4 10.81%

instructor. The descriptive findings over the demographic distribution of the participants are as follows:

The limitation of using a convenience sampling method in this study needs to be recognised since this non-probability sampling strategy may limit the generalisability of the results to other EMI contexts across the world (Dörnyei, 2007).

7.3 Research design

This study adopted a qualitative research design based on narrative frames and semi-structured interviews. Therefore, this research design aims to explore the participants' thoughts and interpretations of professional needs. Concerning this, the study addresses the following research questions:

(1a) What are the EMI instructors' language-related needs?
(1b) What are the EMI instructors' instructional needs?
(2) What components should a professional development program have for EMI instructors?

7.4 Method in detail

7.4.1 *Data collection*

Data were collected through two sources: Narrative frames and semi-structured interviews. Concerning narrative frames (see Appendix A), sentence starters to guide the participants were used (i.e. *When I teach through EMI, I sometimes experience problems in using English. This happens when . . .*). In addition to that, a subgroup of EMI instructors (*n*=10) attended interviews after providing written informed consent. Piloting of the interviews revealed no necessary chances for wording (see Appendix B for the interview protocol). For ethical purposes, pseudonyms were used while referencing the interview data. Interview data were collected in the participants' native language, which is Turkish.

7.4.2 Data analysis

The qualitative data obtained through narrative frames and semi-structured interviews were investigated to determine the EMI instructors' linguistic and pedagogical needs. Therefore, a qualitative content analysis approach was taken.

Narrative frames were first translated by the author (a native Turkish speaker) from Turkish to English and then translated back to Turkish by a second translator that is bilingual in Turkish and English. Both translations were compared so as to provide accuracy in meaning. Second, the researchers read the translated scripts a couple of times to gain familiarity with the content of the narrative frames. Third, grounded theory was adopted through initial, focused and axial coding (Charmaz, 2006). In the initial coding process, the researchers independently coded the data and generated some provisional codes that suited the data. Initial codes were compared in the focused coding stage, and some were selected based on their frequency and significance. In the axial coding stage, the codes that went through initial and focused coding were grouped and synthesised into specific categories following their similar characteristics (see Table 7.2 for the sample coding).

To interpret the narrative frames data precisely, the author coded the transcripts after one month. A high degree of intra-rater reliability was achieved ($k=.93$). Then, the same data were also coded by another researcher and a very good degree of agreement between the coders was found ($k=.91$) (Landis & Koch, 1977).

As for the interview data, thematic content analysis was employed (Thomas, 2006). Interviews were transcribed verbatim, translated into English and back-translated to Turkish to ensure accuracy. Then, each transcript was analysed based on open, axial and selective coding (Corbin & Strauss, 2008). Two independent researchers coded the data line by line and constructed themes based on groups of codes. Accordingly, inter-rater reliability revealed *0.82* agreement between coders, which is sufficient (Miles & Huberman, 1994).

7.4.3 Findings

7.4.3.1 EMI instructors' language needs

Narrative frames and semi-structured interviews were used to investigate EMI instructors' needs regarding English use when they teach through English. In

Table 7.2 Sample coding for narrative frames

Initial coding	Focused coding	Axial coding
Unable to attend daily conversations with students Thinking in Turkish and then translating it into English Pausing a lot	Fluency	Speaking skill

so doing, first, major and sub-themes were derived from the narrative frames. Second, the semi-structured interviews were used to expand on EMI instructors' narratives and provide further information concerning their needs regarding English use.

The qualitative content analysis employed for narrative frames concerning English use resulted in one major theme: The speaking skill of the EMI instructors. The responses provided for the language needs concerning speaking skills address sub-themes: (1) inability to find suitable words, (2) pronunciation and (3) fluency.

Table 7.3 indicates the results of the frequency count of responses (Refs) to the two featured starters (*I sometimes have difficulties concerning English use while teaching through English. This happens when (1)—. Another difficulty I experience is (2)—*).

Inability to find suitable words. EMI instructors' inability to find suitable words while teaching through English is the most frequently mentioned difficulty ($n=20$). Most of them find it difficult to remember and use the exact words appropriately. For example, one of the respondents wrote:

> *I sometimes have difficulties concerning English use while teaching through English. This happens when I try to find the appropriate and comprehensible words for my students. Another difficulty I experience is when I try to tell the details of an experimental setup. I sometimes cannot find the exact words.*
>
> (T3)

Similarly, another respondent stated:

> *I sometimes have difficulties concerning English use while teaching through English. This happens when I try to remember the words. Another difficulty I experience is when I want to use different expressions and words to make the subject more comprehensible.*
>
> (T11)

In addition to that, another respondent said: *I sometimes have difficulties concerning English use while teaching through English. This happens*

Table 7.3 EMI instructors' needs concerning English use

Major theme	Refs (Total number)	Sub-themes	Refs. (Number)
Speaking skills of English	37	Inability to find the suitable words	20
		Fluency	12
		Pronunciation	5

when I want to utter the English equivalent of the terminological words. I can easily remember Turkish terminology, but I have difficulty remembering their English equivalence.

(T15)

This finding was also supported by the interview data, as shown in the following excerpts: '*I have already known a large amount of vocabulary, but my vocabulary use is minimal. I need to improve my active vocabulary*' (Murat). '*I may be provided with explicit instruction about field-specific vocabulary. Thus, it may be easy for me to recognise and recall the vocabulary*' (Ahmet).

Most respondents thought that although they retained vocabulary, they had challenges using the words actively when communicating. Also, they expressed that they could not use a wide range of vocabulary; thus, they reported that they found it difficult to talk about various topics related to the course content.

Fluency. Another most salient sub-theme derived from the narrative frames was the respondents' problems in speaking English fluently when they teach through English. They indicated that they believed they could not speak English on a wide variety of subjects without hesitation. For instance, one of them wrote:

I sometimes have difficulties concerning English use while teaching through English. This happens when I give straightaway examples other than lecture notes that I have prepared beforehand. Another difficulty I experience is that my lecture speeches are not natural English; they are generally mechanical and related to the lecture content. I cannot engage in common interactions with my students apart from the lecture, such as talking about daily life.

(T30)

Echoing this view, another respondent mentioned that he often experienced speaking English fluently and mentioned: '*This happens when I want to give further examples to my students about the subject. I often think in Turkish and then translate my words into English; thus, I always pause when speaking*' (T37).

Along similar lines, the following excerpts also showed that the interviewees thought they would like to improve their speaking skills in terms of fluency: '*I do not have that automatic when I speak English during classes. I pause a lot, which makes me extremely uncomfortable. So, I should be given further assistance about that*' (Alp). '*Although I know the complex grammar rules and vocabulary, I cannot deliver my lecture content smoothly and comfortably. Maybe, I am a perfectionist who is obsessed with accurate utterances. But I can say I am not fluent anyway*' (Fatma).

As a result, some respondents agreed that they had difficulty expressing themselves in English spontaneously and were unable to think in English; thus, they reported they frequently did mental translations from Turkish to English and could not speak smoothly.

Pronunciation. Pronunciation was one of the main themes derived from the interview data. Concerning this, some respondents wrote in narrative frames that they had difficulties pronouncing the English words during instruction. Accordingly, one respondent said: '*I sometimes have difficulties concerning English use while teaching through English. This happens when I pronounce some words, such as mathematical formulations. I cannot remember the exact pronunciation of these formulas*' (T26). Likewise, another respondent stated: '*This happens when I realise I have a thick accent. I cannot pronounce many words correctly when teaching my courses*' (T31).

In parallel thinking, when asked about the language needs of the EMI instructors, one interviewee said: '*I need to have correct English pronunciation. I do not think that my pronunciation is good. Therefore, I often feel hesitant when I teach through English because I fear not being understood by my students*' (Elif).

Another interviewee also emphasised that he needs further improvement in pronouncing English words as he thinks his field entirely relies on oral communication.

> *My field is sociology. We often discuss complex concepts and engage in deep conversations. I need to direct thought-provoking questions to my students. I need to be clear and precise regarding my articulation and pronunciation. I do not feel adequate in this.*
>
> (Hakan)

Finally, the respondents narrated that one of their problem areas in speaking relies on pronunciation. A few respondents mentioned that their pronunciation was not good enough to sound clear and natural.

7.4.3.2   EMI instructors' instructional needs

7.4.3.2.1   NARRATIVE FRAMES

Narrative frames and semi-structured interviews were used to explore EMI instructors' instructional needs when they teach through English. Concerning narrative frames, two featured starters (*In order to improve the quality of EMI classes that I teach, I would like to improve my knowledge and skills on how these classes can be taught. Therefore, I would like to know more about (4)—. That is because (5)—*) were analysed. The results focused on two primary instructional needs: (1) Materials and methods for content delivery ($n=30$) and (2) Enhancing interaction in the EMI classes ($n=7$).

Materials and methods. Concerning materials and methods, one respondent wrote:

> To improve the quality of EMI classes that I teach, I would like to improve my knowledge and skills on how these classes can be taught. Therefore, I would like to know more about oral lecture presentation methods to teach technical content. That is because I want to be more understandable for my students.
>
> (T6)

Similarly, another respondent also mentioned:

> To improve the quality of EMI classes that I teach, I would like to improve my knowledge and skills on how these classes can be taught. Therefore, I would like to know more about developing materials specific to my course. That is because I want my content to become more concrete and digestible
>
> (T23)

Another respondent also wrote:

> In order to improve the quality of EMI classes that I teach, I would like to improve my knowledge and skills on how these classes can be taught. Therefore, I would like to know more about digital teaching techniques. That is because online instruction has become a part of our life.
>
> (T32)

During the interviews, EMI instructors elaborated their opinions on their methodological needs, and some ($n=5$) stated that they needed to improve their knowledge and skills in testing and assessment. They reported that testing and assessment are a vital part of instruction in finding weak and strong student areas. However, the main reason for their need for further improvement in this area was teaching course content in English. As such, they thought that as they delivered the course in English, they were sometimes worried about whether/how well the students comprehended the course. For instance, one respondent explained:

> Students' grammar levels in English may differ because I realise that some students do not fully understand me. For this reason, I direct questions to them to check whether they understand me or not. Therefore, it would be better for me to get further education for learning more in-class assessment practices to pinpoint students' knowledge gaps.
>
> (Sibel)

Echoing this view, another participant emphasised that EMI necessitated a target language use during assessment. She agreed that EMI instructors should use English appropriately when asking questions and preparing test items. She thus said:

> *I need to know good practices of language use in the course of the assessment. This is necessary for students' clear understanding. Therefore, we can be provided training about correct wording in English for assessment practices such as asking questions.*
>
> (Fatma)

Similar to what is expressed in the narrative frames concerning the development of materials and methods, two respondents in the interviews also indicated their need to find out how to accommodate multiple learning styles to increase the students' active participation in the class. They reported that they would like to differentiate the methods and activities of course delivery to grasp the students' attention. Talking about this issue, one respondent said:

> *My course is generally based on lectures. As a result, I mostly use visuals such as slides, but there can be other methods for delivering courses, particularly for English content. Using the same method can be boring for my students and me. Therefore, we should learn more about various methods specifically designed for EMI. This may promote students' interest in the lesson.*
>
> (Alp)

Likewise, another respondent commented:

> *I teach at International Relations, which is mainly based on oral work such as discussions. However, the students are reluctant to express their opinions orally. This may be because they avoid speaking English as they think they can express themselves better in Turkish. Alternatively, this may be because they may have different learning needs, such as visualisation or studying alone. Therefore, I may need to learn different practices to teach multiple learning styles so that I could address their needs.*
>
> (Asya)

Enhancing interaction. Stating the need for more knowledge and skills concerning methods/materials for their EMI classes, several respondents ($n=7$) also indicated in narrative frames that they needed to learn practices to facilitate interaction in their classes. They reported that their students were primarily silent during the class as they were unwilling to speak English, as illustrated in the following narrative frames:

> In order to improve the quality of EMI classes that I teach, I would like to improve my knowledge and skills on how these classes can be taught. Therefore, I would like to know more about ways of creating interaction in English. That is because the students are always silent, and they force me to speak Turkish.
> (T24)

Echoing the same views, another respondent also stated:

> To improve the quality of EMI classes that I teach, I would like to improve my knowledge and skills on how these classes can be taught. Therefore, I would like to know more about how I can enhance active participation. That is because my students remain silent.
> (T27)

Concerning interactive practices, several other respondents ($n=4$) in the interviews specifically reported that they needed to know how to promote group works in EMI classrooms. They thought most of their students were Turkish and were mainly unwilling to speak English during class. Therefore, they argued that they would like to know more about the good practices of encouraging group work. The illustrative excerpts below show their need for creating group works:

> As the instructors and students are mostly Turkish, students generally do not want to speak English during classes. For this reason, we need to promote interaction for better learning. I believe that group work can enable interaction. Thus, I need to know better ways to promote group works in my class.
> (Emre)

> In my class, there are many students with low English proficiency. This results in an unwillingness to speak English. When I direct them questions, my questions generally go unanswered, although I am sure they know the answers. However, they do not want to speak in English as they fear making mistakes due to their low proficiency. Therefore, I think group work may be beneficial for making them speak English as they may have the chance to motivate each other. There must be effective ways of grouping students to motivate them to use English. As an EMI instructor, I need that.
> (Melis)

As a result, EMI instructors communicated their needs centring around developing methods/materials and interactive teaching practices to make their classes more comprehensible and engage the students actively.

7.4.3.3 Professional development program components for EMI instructors

To find out what components should a professional development program include for EMI instructors, narrative frames and semi-structured interviews were used. The qualitative content analysis employed for narrative frames resulted in two major themes: (1) language-related components and (2) pedagogy-related components. Table 7.4 outlines the themes and sub-themes for two starters in the narrative frames (see Starters 3 and 6 in Appendix A). These themes significantly overlapped with the themes derived from semi-structured interviews.

7.4.3.3.1 LANGUAGE-RELATED COMPONENTS

One significant finding was that the EMI instructors narrated their professional needs linked to developing English speaking skills ($n=38$). Concerning this, they reported that they needed to attend academic abroad experiences ($n=18$), speaking clubs to improve their English ($n=10$), and receive education/support on field-specific English ($n=10$).

A high proportion of EMI instructors reported in narrative frames that they must be given opportunities to study abroad or attend academic conferences abroad. Commonly, they thought that if they had more chances of academic abroad experiences, they would develop their English-speaking skills as they could spend time abroad with other English speakers within an academic setting. For example, one respondent wrote: *"We should be sent abroad for at least six months of the academic visit so that we could have the chance to practice English very often. As a result, this will enhance relevant field-specific English vocabulary range"* (T29).

Similarly, another respondent explained: *"The opportunities for attending academic conferences should be increased. In this way, we can make English presentations and practice speaking more and improve pronunciation"*. (T5).

Similarly, during the interviews, all participants ($n=10$) agreed that academic experiences abroad would be highly beneficial in terms of

Table 7.4 Narrative frames analysis results for professional development program components

Major theme	Sub-themes	Refs. (Number)
Language-related components	Academic abroad experiences	18
	Attending speaking courses	10
	Receiving education/support on field-specific English	10
Pedagogy-related components	Receiving an update on teaching methods	30
	Learning communicative techniques for learners	7

improving English speaking skills. Some of them specifically recommended that the professional development program include a period where the EMI instructors study abroad for postgraduate studies. For example, Asya said:

> Studying abroad for a post-doc program should be part of a professional development program for EMI instructors. This would help us improve our English speaking and writing skills if we were sent to a country where English is spoken as a native language. Then, we should always speak English to communicate with academics and manage our daily lives. This will increase the ability to speak with speed and accuracy.

Another common issue related to developing English speaking skills was that EMI instructors thought speaking courses should be provided in their professional development programs. One of the respondents wrote in the narrative frames: '*Speaking courses can be held periodically. These courses may help develop English in terms of speaking smoothly*' (T12).

Similarly, another respondent also wrote: '*I need speaking courses. In a professional development program for us, these courses can highly contribute to my pronunciation. I must brush up on my pronunciation as I easily forget the pronunciation of words*' (T14). Speaking courses were also mentioned during the interviews. Several other interviewees ($n=8$) also believed that attending speaking courses would improve their speaking skills. As one interviewee puts it:

> *I must say that the most effective way of improving English speaking skills is attending a speaking course. Thanks to them, you can practise English, and as a result, you can speak English confidently as you have the chance to speak English with other people.*
>
> (Emre)

Apart from issues related to general English, most of the respondents ($n=10$) also believed they should be provided with a field-specific English education in the professional development programs. They notably stated that specialised terminology should be taught in a communicative setting as they believed this could facilitate recognising and actively using the vocabulary related to their majors. For example, one respondent wrote in narrative frames: '*I need to improve my professional English; therefore, a professional English textbook or sourcebook where there are field-specific words and definitions should be provided*' (T20).

In the same line, another respondent also wrote: '*In a professional development program particularly designed for my field, which is Mathematics, I need to receive training on the pronunciation of the mathematical equations because I hardly read mathematical expressions*' (T21).

As a result, this study shows that language-related components centred around general and field-specific English, and the EMI instructors reported that professional development programs should address those issues.

7.4.3.3.2 PEDAGOGY-RELATED COMPONENTS

A majority of the EMI instructors (n=30) indicated in narrative frames that EMI instructors should need to be provided with the most current approaches. In so doing, they explained that professional development programs should be adapted to different disciplines. For instance, one respondent wrote: '*Concerning this, it would be helpful if I am provided with a professional development program about new and specific methods related to my subject so that I could become more comprehensible to my students*' (T34).

Similarly, one of the respondents in the interviews commented that social sciences and mathematical, physical and life sciences differ in the content to be taught. As a result, she believes that English use and related approaches to deliver this English content need to change, as mentioned in the illustrative excerpt below:

The professional development programs should adapt to the EMI disciplines. Therefore, they should include the most current approaches concerning English use to teach these different disciplines. For example, my department is Philosophy, so it is based heavily on oral communication, such as discussion. Thus, an EMI instructor in this discipline needs to know the current approaches in using English to deliver related content.

(Melis)

The respondents also confirmed in the interviews that they should receive updates about the most current teaching approaches in professional development programs designed for EMI instructors. One of the respondents explained this rationale in her words as follows:

Instructional approaches and methods may change with time. For instance, due to the Covid-19 pandemic, we suddenly had to adapt to remote teaching, and online instruction is still a part of formal education. Maybe, it will be like this forever. However, I do not think that we know exactly how to teach through English online. For example, what should I do in English use in online classes for effective teaching? Or, how should I use English when giving feedback online? We should be informed about methodologies continuously considering the changing pedagogies and approaches.

(Fatma)

Investigating EMI instructors' linguistic and pedagogical needs 107

Apart from the updated methods, the EMI instructors also believed that communication-oriented techniques should be taught in a professional development program for EMI instructors to promote interaction among their students. For instance, one of the respondents wrote in the narrative frames: '*Concerning this, it would be helpful for me if I am provided with a professional development program about how I can promote student talk in English to get my students to interact with each other*' (T36).

Similarly, Ahmet, one of the interviewees, also explained this issue as follows:

In EMI classes which I teach, the students generally opt for speaking Turkish and avoid using English. Maybe, they think that using English is nonsense and that there is no real setting that obliges them to use English when nearly all students with the instructors are Turkish. Most of the time, they are silent when they are not allowed to use Turkish. Therefore, I need to engage them to communicate actively in English. I think that most EMI instructors suffer from this problem. So, it would be better to incorporate communicative techniques in a professional development program for EMI instructors.

Building on Ahmet's comments concerning students' unwillingness to use English during the courses as the classes mostly have Turkish students, Sibel also explained that students' English proficiency level is generally intermediate. Thus, she reported that their oral communication skills should be improved, mainly when they speak in public, as illustrated in the following excerpt:

In a professional development program for EMI instructors, the authorities should consider the students' needs. Because many students do not have higher English proficiency, they cannot effectively speak in class to express their thoughts or discuss them in detail. Therefore, the program content should address this problem by informing EMI instructors about the techniques to encourage communication for students with intermediate or lower proficiency in English.

7.5 Practical lessons learned

7.5.1 *Language and pedagogy-related needs of EMI instructors*

The qualitative analysis of narrative frames and semi-structured interviews showed that EMI instructors' language-related needs were centred around English speaking skills. Specifically, they reported the need to improve their vocabulary range, fluency, and pronunciation to speak comfortably and naturally. This finding resonates with the other studies in EMI literature (see Alhassan, 2021; Banks, 2018). For example, Alhassan (2021) found out that the EMI teachers were reported to have low language proficiency and thus experience difficulty in explaining and describing the subject in depth. Similarly, in Banks' study (2018), EMI lecturers were willing to improve their pronunciation as they were often reported to make pronunciation mistakes. Similar findings show that EMI instructors have language-related problems and thus are keys to guiding EMI teacher development programs. A starting point for this may be explicitly focusing on linguistic competencies in an EMI teacher development program.

Another remarkable finding in this study is that EMI instructors must improve their instructional practices, particularly testing and assessment. EMI instructors thought they needed to know accurate ways of asking questions in English because they were often worried about the comprehensibility of their questions. This finding is echoed in the study by Abouzeid (2021). She pointed out that the EMI instructors might need to adjust the types of assessment to measure the content knowledge, which ended up with a narrow evaluation of the subject due to the students' low proficiency. That means she reported that EMI instructors might refrain from giving comprehensive writing assignments because they believed the students did not have good proficiency in English. Therefore, they might not write responses that could reflect their proper understanding of the subject. This clearly shows that EMI instructors need to know alternative ways of testing and assessing EMI students. Otherwise, they may avoid asking questions that require the students to produce open-ended responses because of their low English proficiency. As a result, they may ask the same type of questions, such as selected responses, which may hinder the assessment of the actual performance of EMI students.

In addition to testing and assessment, EMI instructors reported that they needed to know how to create group work and teach multiple learning styles. This finding implies that they would like to enhance interaction for their students. As Evans and Morrison (2011) indicated, most EMI classes suffer from a lack of interaction due to the imposition of the use of English. Therefore, this present study shows that EMI instructors pursue encouraging classroom interactions. As the EMI instructors in this study felt that most students are likely to stay silent, forming group work may be a remedy to this problem. Groups works as an EMI practice is significant in allowing students to use English actively in class (Fenton-Smith et al., 2017). Another alternative could be using efficient teaching methods according to the students' learning styles. In parallel thinking, Bakkar (2021) and Fenton-Smith et al. (2017) also indicate that EMI teaching should be designed following the students' diverse skills and learning styles. Therefore, this finding is key to guiding EMI program developers as it highlights the need to teach various communicative techniques and methods to EMI instructors to cater to EMI students' needs, thereby facilitating classroom interaction.

7.5.2 *Professional development program components for EMI instructors*

The narrative frames and semi-structured interviews revealed that the ideal professional development program for EMI instructors should improve their

English-speaking skills by incorporating speaking courses and providing academic experiences abroad. These findings are similar to several studies in the related literature (e.g. Galloway & Ruegg, 2022; Mancho-Bares & Arno-Macia, 2017; Piquer-Piriz & Castellano-Risco, 2021). Similar findings highlight a need for more English language support for EMI instructors. Therefore, professional development programs should include language courses, mainly speaking and training abroad, such as exchange programs. This may enhance the language proficiency of the EMI instructors.

Another remarkable finding from this study is that EMI instructors believed they should be provided with a field-specific English education in the professional development programs. This finding resonates with the study by Morell et al. (2022). Accordingly, they implemented a professional development program for EMI teachers where they offered a course of subject-specific English based on the teachers' professional needs. Likewise, Pecorari et al. (2011) also emphasised that EMI instructors prioritise subject-specific terminology, unlike general English. An implication for the program developers for EMI instructors may be explicitly incorporating subject-specific English while providing language support.

In addition, as for the pedagogy-related components, the EMI instructors claimed that an ideal professional development program should teach EMI instructors various communicative techniques to be used in the classes and provide a regular update on teaching methods. They thought that if they learned more about the communicative techniques and current methods, they could encourage classroom talk among the students and engage them actively. This result is in line with studies by Tsui (2017) and Ellison et al. (2017). They suggest that pedagogical support should be given to EMI instructors in a professional development program by providing knowledge about methodology and strategies. One pedagogical implication of this finding could be to augment and provide methodological and strategical assistance for EMI instructors in professional development programs.

7.6 Concluding summary

This study specifically examined EMI instructors' linguistic and pedagogical needs and set out to find out the components of an ideal professional development program based on the perspectives of EMI instructors. The instructors recognised the need for improvement in some areas. Among them, the linguistic needs relied on the improvement of speaking skills of English. In contrast, pedagogical needs focused on methodological support, particularly testing/assessment, formation of group works and teaching multiple learning styles. Therefore, there is a clear need to raise EMI instructors' knowledge and skills concerning general language and subject-specific language. Second, EMI instructors needed to gain an understanding of and enhance the skills of methodologies about content teaching through English. Therefore, this current study provides insights into the development of a professional development program as it clearly shows the pedagogical and linguistic needs and the content of a potential program for EMI instructors.

References

Abouzeid, R. (2021). Aligning perceptions with reality: Lebanese EMI instructor perceptions of students' writing proficiency. *English for Specific Purposes, 63*, 45–58. https://doi.org/10.1016/j.esp.2021.03.001

Alhassan, A. (2021). Challenges and professional development needs of EMI lecturers in Omani higher education. *Sage Open, 11*(4). https://doi.org/10.1177/21582440211061527

Bakkar, B. B. (2021, April). Challenges in teaching literature in EMI to EFL speaking students at university level: Instructors' perception. *3rd world conference on research*, Prague, Czech Republic. www.dpublication.com/wp-content/uploads/2021/04/4-80013.pdf

Banks, M. (2018). Exploring EMI lectures' attitudes and needs. *EPiC Series in Language and Linguistics, 3*, 19–26.

Barkhuizen, G., & Wette, R. (2008). Narrative frames for investigating the experiences of language teachers. *System, 36*, 372–387. https://doi.org/10.1016/j.system.2008.02.002

Block, D., & Moncada-Comas, B. (2019). English-medium instruction in higher education and the ELT gaze: STEM lecturers' self-positioning as NOT English language teachers. *International Journal of Bilingual Education and Bilingualism 25*(2). https://doi.org/10.1080/13670050.2019.1689917

Breeze, R., & Roothooft, H. (2021). Using the L1 in university-level EMI: Attitudes among lecturers in Spain. *Language Awareness, 30*(2), 195–215. https://doi.org/10.1080/09658416.2021.1903911

Charmaz, K. (2006). *Constructing grounded theory: A practical guide through qualitative analysis*. Sage.

Corbin, J., & Strauss, A. (2008). *Basics of qualitative research*. Sage.

Dörnyei, Z. (2007). *Research methods in applied linguistics*. Oxford University Press.

Ellison, M., Araujo, S., Correira, M., & Vieira, F. (2017). Teachers' perceptions of need in EAP and ICLHE contexts. In J. Valcke & R. Wilkinson (Eds.), *Integrating content and language in higher education: Perspectives on professional practice* (pp. 59–76). Peter Lang Publishing Group.

Evans, S., & Morrison, B. (2011). Meeting the challenges of English-medium higher education: The first-year experience in Hong Kong. *English for Specific Purposes, 30*(3), https://doi.org/10.1016/j.esp.2011.01.001

Fenton-Smith, B., Stillwell, C., & Dupuy, R. (2017). Professional development for EMI: Exploring Taiwanese lecturers' needs. In B. Fentom-Smith, P. Humpreys, & I. Walkinshaw (Eds.), *English medium instruction in higher education in Asia-Pacific: From policy to pedagogy* (pp. 195–217). Multilingual Education.

Fortanet-Gomez, I. (2020). The dimensions of EMI in the international classroom: Training teachers for the future university. In M. Sánchez-Pérez (Ed.), *Teacher training for English-medium instruction in higher education* (pp. 1–20). IGI Global.

Galloway, N., & Ruegg, R. (2020). The provision of student support on English medium instruction programmes in Japan and China. *Journal of English for Academic Purposes, 45*. https://doi.org/10.1016/j.jeap.2020.100846

Galloway, N., & Ruegg, R. (2022). English medium instruction (EMI) lecturer support needs in Japan and China. *System, 105,* https://doi.org/10.1016/j.system.2022.102728

Geertz, C. (1973). *The interpretation of cultures: Selected essays.* Basic Books.

Gundermann, S. (2013). *English-medium instruction: Modelling the role of the native speaker in a lingua franca context.* Albert-Ludwigs-Universität Freiburg.

Hu, J., & Wu, P. (2020). Understanding English language learning in tertiary English-medium instruction contexts in China. *System, 93.* https://doi.org/10.1016/j.system.2020.102305

Huang, H., & Curle, S. (2021). Higher education medium of instruction and career prospects: An exploration of current and graduated Chinese students' perceptions. *Journal of Education and Work 34*(3). https://doi.org/10.1080/13639080.2021.1922617

Kırkgöz, Y. (2009). Globalisation and English language policy in Turkey. *Educational Policy, 23*(5), 663–684. https://doi.org/10.1177/0895904808316319

Landis, J. R., & Koch, G. G. (1977). The measurement of observer agreement for categorical data. *Biometrics, 33*(1), 159–174. https://doi.org/10.2307/2529310

Legal Gazette. (1982). *Constitution of the Republic of Turkey.* https://www5.tbmm.gov.tr//develop/owa/tc_anayasasi.maddeler?p3=42

Mancho-Bares, G., & Arno-Macia, E. (2017). EMI lecturer training programmes and academic literacies: A critical insight from ESP. *ESP Today, 5*(2), 266–290. https://doi.org/10.18485/esptoday.2017.5.2.7

Miles, M. B., & Huberman, A. M. (1994). *Qualitative data analysis: An expanded sourcebook.* Sage.

Morell, T., Aleson-Carbonell, M., & Escabias-Lloret, P. (2022). Prof-teaching: An English-medium instruction professional development program with a digital, linguistic and pedagogical approach. *Innovation in Language Learning and Teaching 16*(4–5). https://doi.org/10.1080/17501229.2022.2052298

O'Dowd, R. (2018). The training and accreditation of teachers for English medium instruction: an overview of practice in European universities. *International Journal of Bilingual Education and Bilingualism, 21*(5), 553–563. https://doi.org/10.1080/13670050.2018.1491945

Pecorari, D., Shaw, P., Irvine, A., & Malmström, H. (2011). English for academic purposes at Swedish universities: Teachers' objectives and practices. *Iberica, 22,* 55–78.

Piquer-Piriz, A. M., & Castellano-Risco, I. O. (2021). Lecturers' training needs in EMI programmes: Beyond language competence. *Alicante Journal of English Studies, 34,* 83–105.

Rahman, M. M., Reshmin, L., Amin, E., & Karim, A. (2022). The influence of apprenticeship of observation on business teacher's beliefs and attitudes towards English-medium instruction: A case study. *Social Sciences & Humanities, 30*(1), 171–189. https://doi.org/10.47836/pjssh.30.1.10

Roothooft, H. (2022). Spanish lecturers' beliefs about English medium instruction: STEM versus humanities. *International Journal of Bilingual Education and Bilingualism, 25*(2), 627–640. https://doi.org/10.1080/13670050.2019.1707768

Thomas, D. R. (2006). A general inductive approach for analysing qualitative evaluation data. *American Journal of Evaluation, 27*(2), 237–246. https://doi.org/10.1177/1098214005283748

Tsui, C. (2017). EMI teacher development programs in Taiwan. In W. Tsou & S. M. Kao (Eds.), *English as a medium of instruction in higher education: Implementations and classroom practices in Taiwan* (pp. 165–182). Springer.

Viet, N. G. (2012). Narrative frames: Case study. In R. Barnard & A. Burns (Eds.), *Researching language teacher cognition and practice: International case studies* (pp. 48–58). Multilingual Matters.

Webster, L., & Mertova, P. (2007). *Using narrative inquiry as a research method: An introduction to using critical event narrative analysis in research on learning and teaching.* Routledge.

Wit, H. D., & Altbach, P. G. (2021). Internationalisation in higher education: Global trends and recommendations for its future. *Policy Reviews in Higher Education, 5*(1), 28–46. https://doi.org/10.1080/23322969.2020.1820898

Appendix A
Narrative frames for language and instructional-related needs of EMI instructors

When I teach through EMI, I sometimes experience problems in using English. This happens when (1)—. Another difficulty I experience is (2)—. Therefore, it will be beneficial for my professional development if the following steps are taken (3)—. In order to improve the quality of EMI classes that I teach, I would like to improve my knowledge and skills on how these classes can be taught. Therefore, I would like to know more about (4)—. That is because (5)—. Concerning this, it would be helpful for me if I am provided with a professional development program about (6)—

Appendix B
Semi-structured interviews protocol

1. What are your professional needs concerning language use when teaching through English?
2. What are your professional needs concerning teaching methodologies?
3. What do you think the components should be in a development program for EMI instructors?

8 Engaged methodological approach in the study of language ideologies in EMI policies

Prem Phyak, Nani Babu Ghimire and Mohan Singh Saud

8.1 Introduction

This chapter builds on the idea of 'engaged ethnography' (Davis & Phyak, 2016) in language education policy to discuss the methodological approaches to study language ideologies in EMI policies. We draw on three different cases representing diverse multilingual settings of Nepal. Our goal in the chapter is to discuss how different engaged methods can be used to explore language ideologies in EMI policies by engaging different stakeholders impacted by the policies. Our ontological perspectives are shaped by the assumptions that EMI policy studies should pay attention to language ideology not just as an analytical concept but as a tool to engage multiple actors in understanding policies' sociopolitical meanings and impacts on their lived experiences. The engagements we discuss in the chapter are dialogic and critical in nature and engage the participants not just to provide data but to be critically reflective in analysing language ideological meanings of EMI policies.

8.2 Understanding engagement in our research

Engagement in this chapter should be understood as a process through which researchers engage participants in critical dialogues. It requires researchers' own participation in critical understanding about different forms of dominations with the participants (Mathers & Navelli, 2007). Engaged researchers do not distance themselves from the topic of discussion rather they create space for the participants to share their ideas and opinions about ideological meanings of EMI policies. In other words, 'engagement' should be taken as an invitation to a dialogue for critical discussion on ideological aspects of EMI policies. It is a 'reflective space . . . for a deeper understanding of the views and experiences from the field' (Ghorashi & Wels, 2009, p. 246). In this space, researchers and participants collectively develop critical understanding about sociopolitical meanings of EMI policies.

DOI: 10.4324/9781003375531-9

Critical engagement approach embraces the philosophy of ethnography as an 'anti-hegemonic science' (Hymes, 1996) and 'democratic engagement' (Fine, 2002). We discuss how this perspective offers critical insights into not only understanding but also building awareness about language ideological meanings of EMI policies. Engaged research upholds the view that researchers should collectively engage participants in the critical analyses of power relations, language hierarchies and marginalisation of languages (Davis & Phyak, 2016). Dialogue is a key method in engaged research. It engages both participants and researchers in a situated understanding and exploration of EMI policy in local contexts. In this chapter, we discuss how we adapted dialogic engagement by using three methods: case study, critical ethnography and ethnographic monitoring. Our argument is that EMI policy studies should go beyond data collection and analysis process and pay attention to engaging teachers (and other actors) to analyse language ideological issues and build critical awareness about the impacts (sociopolitical, linguistic, and educational etc.) of EMI policy. Such a process will help us transform discriminatory language policies from the bottom-up by helping teachers develop their ideological awareness and agency to negotiate dominant language policies and ideologies and create just and multilingual policies.

We define dialogic engagement as a reflective process where the participants and researchers collectively explore and analyse language ideological issues concerning EMI policy. For us, dialogue is a collaborative space where both researchers and participants share their voices, beliefs, struggles and the narratives of teaching in EMI schools. It is locally situated and grounded in the context where the participants have lived. The dialogical engagement provides both participants and researchers with a safe and open space to discuss how EMI policies and their ideological impacts can be questioned and transformed. We do not just collect data but use them to engage our participants in unravelling language ideologies to build their critical awareness about sociopolitical meanings of EMI policy. The locally situated dialogues not only respect the participants' knowledge about local complexities but also help them develop agency and awareness about language education policies.

8.3 A brief ideological context of EMI policy in Nepal

Nepal is a multilingual and multiethnic country. More than 130 languages are spoken across more than 60 different indigenous and 125 ethnic/caste groups. Despite this linguistic cultural diversity, the state's language policies have historically been exclusionary for Indigenous/ethnic minority people. The public spheres such as education and government offices are dominated by Nepali and English languages. The historical domination of linguistic nationalism has constructed and promoted Nepali as a sole national language of the nation-state. This ideology has erased the space of Indigenous/minority languages from education. Although there are policies, at least in text, for mother tongue education, schools are still using Nepali and English as mediums of instruction. Mother tongue education policy is hardly implemented in schools throughout the country.

The use of English as a medium of instruction is historically linked with elitism. When the nation-state had promoted a one-nation-one-language policy for the public (including education) till 1990, the state had allowed missionaries and the British Government to establish English-medium schools for the elites and foreigners. These schools have played a critical role to construct the discourse of EMI as the sign of quality education in the public sphere. After the restoration of a liberal democratic system in 1990, the state adopted a neoliberal ideology to reform public policies. This ideology contributed to the emergence of private schools, mainly in urban areas, to cater to the needs of parents from relatively high socioeconomic status (Phyak & Bui, 2014). English is implemented as a de facto medium of instruction in private schools. The use of local languages including Nepali (except in language classes) is banned to create an English-only environment (Phyak & Sharma, 2021). The language behaviours of students and teachers are consistently monitored, and they are punished if they break the English-speaking rule within the school premises (Thebe Limbu, 2021). Although EMI policy was not legal until 2006, private schools were using it as a commodity and were collecting expensive fees from parents.

Following the state's language policy, public schools are historically known as Nepali medium schools. As the number of private schools is increasing across the country, these schools face an increased pressure to enrol more students. This divisive policy has constructed a hegemonic ideology of EMI as a major symbol of quality education (Phyak, 2016). Ghimire's (2019) study shows that 'the public consider English medium schools to be better than others [Nepali medium] and they send their children to private schools in the name of quality education' (p. 148). His analysis reveals that the English medium has been 'a fashion' and it has posed a huge pressure for public schools to adopt EMI policy. Research has shown that there is a growing trend of adopting EMI policy in public schools to compete with private schools and increase student number (Phyak & Sah, 2022).

The government eventually revised its educational act in 2006 to legitimise EMI policy. According to the revised policy, Nepali or English or both languages can be used as a medium of instruction in public schools. This policy not only legalised the de facto EMI policy of private schools but also reproduced the ideology of English medium as quality education. Moreover, the policy allowed public schools to introduce EMI policy. At the same time, the government has been consistently focusing on mother tongue education in its policy documents. In the revised policy, it is stated that mother tongue can be used as a medium of instruction for the basic level of education (Grades 1–8). However, both public and private schools throughout the country are focusing on EMI policy. The leaders of local government are also encouraging public schools to implement EMI policy for quality education. However, studies have consistently shown that this policy is not only promoting linguistic inequalities but also posing challenges for effective teaching-learning engagement (Phyak, 2016). In the remainder of the chapter, we discuss our methodological approaches to engage teachers in analysing multiple ideologies around the issue of EMI policy.

8.4 Using case study for a situated engagement

Mohan (the third author) has used a multiple case study approach (Yin, 2003) to engage teachers in critical dialogues to explore divergent language ideologies in EMI policies. He used multimethod approaches such as interview, observation, diary writing, and field notes to understand the context and practices of EMI policy in three public schools in the Kailali district of Far Western Province of Nepal. All the schools are multilingual, representing the students coming from Indigenous Rana Tharu communities and the emigrants from the hill districts and rural villages who speak different mother tongues such as Doteli and Achhami. The schools have adopted a dual medium of instruction (Nepali and English) policy. Mohan is particularly interested in engaging teachers in dialogues to understand why public schools are adopting segregated EMI policies. Mohan's study does not simply analyse the policy documents but uses them to engage teachers in critical discussions on the impacts and ideologies of EMI policies.

Mohan's interest in engaged research emerges from his close observation of EMI policies in the case study schools. He noticed that there has been a social divide because of EMI policy. In all three case study schools, Nepali medium of instruction (NMI) and EMI classes are run in different infrastructures and by different teachers. In one of the selected schools, EMI classes are conducted in the morning shift while the NMI classes are taught in the day shift. Although the government policy does not allow public schools to collect fees, these schools are charging fees to the students to pay their teachers in EMI sections. Only the parents who can afford fees admit their children in EMI classes and those who cannot afford to admit their children in NMI classes. This situation has prompted Mohan to engage teachers in critical dialogue to help them and himself understand sociopolitical meanings of EMI policy. He also observed that EMI is seen as a capital by parents (Ojha, 2018; Sah & Li, 2018; Saud, 2020a) without knowing its educational dimensions. In his discussion with teachers, he found that even teachers are reproducing the ideology of English as a symbol of quality education. Yet, he noticed that both teachers and students have been struggling hard to participating in teaching-learning activities due to English language barriers.

Mohan's dialogic engagement with teachers begins with a general reflection session to share what he has learned from the observation of classes and discussion with teachers. For example, before he had a dialogue with teachers,

Mohan quickly shared how students were almost silent in EMI classes. Only a few were saying like 'Yes, sir; Yes, mam' while the teachers were teaching but others would not speak anything. There was no interaction at all in class. The teachers mostly explain the subject matter in Nepali rather than English in EMI classes. So, Mohan asks

Mohan: Why do you use Nepali in EMI classes?
T1: If I explain everything in English, students cannot understand clearly.
Mohan: If you have to teach in Nepali why do you think this school has introduced EMI?
T1: Students in private boarding schools get high marks and good results. Seeing this, school administration also wanted to provide quality education by competing with private schools.

As Mohan raises questions, teachers (e.g. T1 above) become more critical about EMI policies. For example, T1 states that they have implemented the policy not because teaching in English is an effective pedagogy, but because the school administration thinks that EMI would provide students with quality education. In the dialogue, Mohan also shares how contents can be better understood in learners' familiar languages (Perez, & Alieto, 2018; Simasiku et al., 2015; Suliman, 2014). In order to engage teachers in more critical dialogue, he shares with the teachers about how research has shown the importance of students' mother tongue in education (Brock-Utne, 2010; Saud, 2022). In other words, he was not only collecting data but also sharing the knowledge from the field and research studies to scaffold the dialogic engagements. For example, in the following excerpt, he would like to engage teachers in assessing whether EMI policy can help to provide quality education:

Mohan: How do you think that EMI can provide quality education, if students do not understand your instruction?
T2: I personally don't think that EMI provides quality education.
Mohan: So, why the schools are implementing this?
T2: EMI is considered as a matter of prestige for public schools. But if students do not understand what you are teaching there is no quality education. I studied in a Nepali medium school. I was taught in Nepali in college. I do not have adequate English language proficiency. Textbooks are in English, but I mostly teach in Nepali. I mix Nepali and English.

The dialogic engagement provides teachers with space for critical and open discussions on EMI policy. As seen earlier, teachers consider EMI as 'a matter of prestige' but not a helpful policy for quality education. T2 questions the ideology of EMI as quality education and argues that if students do not understand what teachers are teaching there is 'no quality education'. With this, teachers become more critical and reflexive about their own English competence, which is not adequate for teaching all content subjects in English. As the teachers become critical, Mohan asks questions about the impact of EMI policy on the local language ecology. He first shares his understanding about local language situation and linguistic backgrounds of the students in local schools. He also highlights how language rights (Skutnabb-Kangas, 2010) are important for socialisation and sense of belonging. He talks briefly about the constitutional provisions and research findings and raises very locally situated questions about the impact of EMI policy.

Mohan: We have students from different language backgrounds here. But they are not allowed to use their mother tongues. Do not you think that this policy is erasing local mother tongues?

T3: People give priority to Nepali or English only. Local or indigenous languages are limited to only grandparents. There is the possibility of local languages being disappeared if they are not taught in school.

Mohan: Can the school teach them?

T3: It can, but mother tongue education is not perceived positively. People think that English is everything these days.

Mahan's deeper understanding about the linguistic situation and pedagogical practices of the schools help him engage teachers and himself in critical dialogue. He would ask follow-up questions and contribute to the dialogue by sharing what he has observed in the schools and what he has read in the existing literature. The dialogue on language rights clearly indicates that teachers develop critical awareness about how EMI has been a hegemonic ideology in the local context. Mohan usually concludes each dialogue session with a summary of what was discussed. For the language rights session, he also shared what he thought about the impact of EMI policy on local language ecology. He drew on his own (Saud, 2020a, p. 32) and other scholars' work (e.g. Crystal, 2002; Gutiérrez Estrada & Schecter, 2018; Khaled, 2020; Skutnabb-Kangas, 2010) to help teachers think about how EMI policy would erase local languages.

Mohan's overall research design adopts a deductive approach. The questions for engagement are drawn from the school context. The case study (Yin, 2003) has given him critical space for engagement with teachers. The dialogues are recorded, transcribed and analysed thematically (Braun & Clarke, 2006).

8.5 Critical ethnography as engaged research

Nani Babu (the second author) adopts a critical ethnographic approach (Thomas, 1993) to engage teachers in understanding the ideologies of EMI policy in the Sindhuli district. The district is ethnically, culturally, linguistically, and socially heterogeneous. Three schools, Shrikantha Secondary School (SSS), Mahabharat Secondary School (MSS) and Dharmachakra Secondary School (DSS) (all pseudo-names), were selected for the study and six teachers

Engaged research method in EMI policy 121

participated in dialogic engagement sessions. Multiple methods such as participant observation, field notes, artefacts documentation and in-depth interviews were used to collect data. The participant classroom observations focused particularly on silencing and power relations as seen in teachers' use of English, teacher–student interactions, content understanding and student responses. The contextual details were documented by using field notes. Nani Babu also collected written artefacts such as school-community demographic records, academic profile, EMI policy documents, the minutes of the management committee, textbooks, lesson plans, students' homework, notebooks, schoolwork and test papers, and teachers' correction and feedback during his study.

All the ethnographic data were later used as resource for critical dialogue to analyse teachers' own ideologies about EMI policies. Such dialogical engagements focused on ideological analyses of ethnographic data about EMI policy in schools. For example, Nani Babu observed Abhimanyu's (one EMI teacher) class and found that the teacher read the contents given in the textbook and tried to interpret the text in English, but he could not because of the lack of adequate English vocabulary and grammatical competence. The students also could not speak in English—they mostly remained silent. After class observation, Nani Babu had a dialogue with Abhimanyu for an hour:

Nani Babu: I saw that it was not quite easy to teach in English. You were using Nepali throughout the class. Why?
Abhimanyu: It makes class interactive, and we can discuss the content of lessons openly.
Nani Babu: Can you give me one example?
Abhimanyu: One day, I was teaching Social Studies at grade three. The topic was 'Formation and function of Ward committee of Rural Municipality'. I read the text, but the students did not understand. Then, I asked them, '[D]o you have '*wadākāryālaya* (ward office) in your village?' They said 'yes'. I asked a student to talk about her *wadāsamiti* (ward committee) in Nepali. She told her experiences of recent local level elections.
Nani Babu: But I saw that students are mostly silent in the classroom.
Abhimanyu: Yes. If we teach in English, they remain silent. They cannot speak in English. It's unfair for them.

In Nani Babu's study schools, there is a widely held ideology that EMI policy helps to improve students' English. But teachers do not use English while teaching content subjects because of a lack of adequate proficiency in English. The students hardly understand and speak English. Therefore, they use students' mother tongue in class. But teachers consider such practices as a deficient pedagogy. Nani Babu engages teachers in understanding the importance of using students' mother tongues in the classroom. For this, he shared his own English language learning and teaching experiences and highlighted the findings from previous research. He was not only collecting data but also helping teachers understand the ideologies of EMI policy and their impacts on students' learning. As seen in the above excerpt, Nani Babu focuses on how EMI policy has made students silent in the classroom. As he engages the teachers in dialogues, they become critical about EMI policy and show their agency to resist a monolingual ideology and create translanguaging space in the classroom. The dialogic engagement helps them recognise the use of students' mother tongue as a legitimate practice.

Nani Babu: Do you think learners' mother tongue is necessary?
Abhimanyu: Yes. It helps them draw on their own experiences. They understand and learn new content knowledge more efficiently.

As teachers embrace the use of mother tongue as a legitimate pedagogical practice, they also become critical about the relevance of EMI policy. Nani Babu and the teachers discussed how EMI classroom pedagogies have been limiting learning. They discussed the meaning of the teachers reading the English texts and translating them into Nepali. Nani Babu shared some major anecdotes from the classroom and invited teachers to share their thoughts. For example, building on Abhimanyu's class where he dominantly uses Nepali to teach social studies, he wanted to know how the teacher thinks about the relevance of EMI policy.

Nani Babu: If EMI is an issue for effective teaching and learning, why do schools run after it?
Abhimanyu: The school management committee imposed us to teach in English medium.
Nani Babu: Can't you deny it?
Abhimanyu: No. Teachers have nothing to say. There is a strong mentality that EMI is same as quality education. The public believe that EMI policy enhances students' English abilities, and they can get a good job to survive. Moreover, they think that EMI policy would help them find many opportunities in foreign countries. But it's just a mentality, I think. Students are not learning both content and English effectively. It's a reality.

Rather than considering data as an end, Nani Babu uses them to collectively understand and explore, with teachers, language ideologies in EMI policies. Teachers were engaged in reflecting on their own language practices in the classroom in relation to EMI policy. Nani Babu and teachers listen to the recorded interviews and read the transcripts together. Nani Babu facilitates the discussion by posing the questions (that emerge from the data) related to sociopolitical conditions and the impacts of EMI policies on the local context. In critical ethnography, power relations and inequalities are major concepts to explore. Nani Babu posed the questions about how EMI policies are creating linguistic inequalities and social injustice in local contexts to the teachers. The questions were drawn from teachers' own experiences they had shared with him during the interviews. The discussions were transcribed and analysed by using a thematic analysis method (Braun & Clarke, 2006) which includes the entire process of identifying, analysing, and reporting the patterns (themes) within data.

What is more striking in Nani Babu's case is that through dialogic engagement teachers develop critical awareness about their own language policies and practices. While reflecting on their own practices, they relate their own struggles and ideologies of teaching in an EMI school to broader sociopolitical conditions. The dialogic engagement shows that most teachers have been critical about EMI policies.

8.6 Ethnographic monitoring as engagement

Prem (the first author) uses Hymesian 'ethnographic monitoring' (Hymes, 1980) to engage teachers in ideological analyses in EMI policies. He draws on 'engage ethnography' (Davis & Phyak, 2016) to build critical awareness of teachers about language ideological issues in EMI policy. In Hymesian ethnographic monitoring, researchers (ethnographers) first discuss with the teachers to identify and understand the issues around language. Second, researchers closely observe the practices and behaviours of different actors (e.g. teachers). They focus on how the issues are being practised in the classroom, school and beyond. This step provides ideas for real-life situations of the issues. The context, actors, activities, resources and language practices are all important dimensions to consider in this step. More strikingly, researchers engage teachers in sharing their narratives related to the issues to understand their voices. In the third step, the findings of the study are shared with the teachers and relevant stakeholders. This step is important in engaged research as it not only recognises the contribution of the teachers but engages them and researchers in the planning of the future activities.

Prem uses 'ethnographically grounded dialogue' (Phyak, 2016) to expand the scope of ethnographic monitoring to engage teachers in critical dialogues about EMI policies in one of the rural schools located in an Indigenous Limbu community. This method builds on a dialogic approach (Freire, 1970) to engage teachers in becoming ideologically aware of the issues and impacts of EMI policy in their school and community. As in Hymes' ethnographic monitoring, first, Prem talked to the teachers, principals and students about their lived experiences of the EMI policy and how it impacts on teaching-learning processes, identities and local linguistic ecology. For this, he had a series of individual and group discussions with the teachers and students. Some discussions were formally organised in the school while most discussions were held informally outside the school. After that, Prem observed the classes, analysed textbooks and other artefacts such as students' writing samples, teachers' feedback, and test papers. Some classes were audio- and video-recorded. But most classroom observation data were documented as field notes.

The major component in engaged research is dialogue. Building on Freire (1970), Prem used dialogue as a critical reflective process in which the teachers and himself were engaged in analysing the ideological meaning of EMI policies and practices. In dialogic engagement, teachers critically evaluated their own practices and offered multiple perspectives and ideologies, about EMI policy. As the teachers reflected on their own practices, they became open to share their own and students' struggles and experiences of teaching and learning in EMI policy. In other words, ethnographically grounded dialogue offered them with an open and critical space for both the teachers and researcher (Prem) to discuss the sociopolitical and educational meanings of the EMI policy in both the local and national contexts. Prem did not only play the role of a researcher observing and recording the dialogue, but also participated in each dialogue as one of the members sharing what he observed in the classroom and beyond. He also facilitated the dialogues by posing questions and providing the context of pedagogical practices in the classroom and linking them to the local and national contexts. The questions for dialogues were not predetermined rather they emerged mostly from the classroom observations. The general questions discussed in the dialogues were as follows:

- How do you assess your own teaching in EMI policy? How do you feel? Do you feel comfortable delivering the lessons in English?
- Why were you allowing the students to use or not to use their mother tongues?
- Why were the students not speaking in class? What made them silent?
- Why were you asking students to speak in their mother tongues?
- Why do you think that the schools are adopting EMI policy?
- How relevant is EMI policy in the school and local community?
- You said EMI policy is a fashion, but how? Why?
- You were just reading the textbook, but students hardly understood what you were reading. Can you explain why?
- I have seen the test papers. Most students cannot read and understand test items. What's your opinion about it?

At the centre of critical dialogues were the teachers' own narratives that helped them share their lived experiences, voices, struggles and beliefs about the EMI policy and practices in the school. In the dialogic engagement, the teachers openly discussed how the policy has serious impacts on their own identity, students' learning engagement and the ecology of language. The teachers agreed that the policy has 'no educational meaning', but it is taken as the 'copy of private schools' policies'. Some teachers claimed that 'it's been a burden and waste of time explaining topics and lessons in English' and argued that the policy is 'just like a fashion'.

One important aspect of Prem's dialogic engagement with the teachers was the building of critical praxis (Freire, 1970). As the teachers were being reflective about the impacts of the EMI policy, they also discussed how they could help their students learn effectively. First, the teachers were not happy about the implementation of the EMI policy. For them, the EMI policy, as one teacher said, is 'just like a slogan with no relevance for them and students'. Most teachers agreed that they use translanguaging to help students understand the lessons and interact in the classroom. During the dialogic engagement, they said that the EMI policy has 'failed' not only students but also teachers. For example, one teacher questioned 'how can we teach content subjects in English? What's the use of EMI policy if it creates more problems for both teachers and students?'

8.7 Conclusion

In this chapter, we have discussed how EMI policies can be studied by using an engaged approach (Phyak, 2021). We keep dialogical engagement at the centre of our methods. We use Freire's (1970) concept of dialogue to engage the teachers who are imposed to teach content subjects in English. As discussed earlier, we use the dominant methods such as case study and ethnography just to collect the experiences and realities to engage teachers in locally situated analyses of language ideologies in EMI policies. We see dialogue as an open, flexible and critical space for understanding, resisting and transforming language ideologies. Therefore, we do not recommend and follow any defined structured research methodology for dialogic engagement. From a Freirean perspective, dialogue is not 'simpl[y] the descriptions of an interactive exchange between people, but a normative definition of how human relationships should be formed—namely, on the basis of equality, respect and a commitment to the authentic interests of participants' (Renshaw, 2004, p. 1). As discussed earlier, we have considered teachers as the 'living members of communities with histories and cultural resources that need to be understood and respected' (Renshaw, 2004, p. 1). We have not imposed our own ideologies, but rather we have contributed to dialogues by sharing our own knowledge and reflections on classroom pedagogies and language practices in schools.

The engaged approach does not simply collect data rather it uses them as a resource to engage participants in the critique of EMI policy. Keeping dialogue at the centre, it pays attention to unravelling and resisting unequal power relations, marginalisation, and linguistic inequalities. Our engaged approach focuses on collaborative dialogues to help teachers connect their own lived experiences (teaching) with macro sociopolitical conditions of EMI policies. For us, engaged research is an act of dialogue (Davis & Phyak, 2016) that is grounded in the 'authentic experiences' of marginalisation and inequalities. It is a bottom-up and participatory process to examine ideological meanings of language policies and practices (Phyak, 2021). We see it as a form of commitment (of course, long-term) for social justice by creating a 'reflective space . . . for a deeper understanding of the views and experiences from the field' (Ghorashi & Wels, 2009, p. 246). We conclude by arguing that EMI researchers should not just collect and analyse data rather they should engage participants (teachers, parents, students etc.) in critical dialogue to analyse ideologies that shape EMI policies. Without doing so, we may reproduce the hegemonic ideologies of monolingual English and contribute to the erasure of local multilingualism. Our approach may look odd and messy because we see engaged research as an unfinished and unstructured approach. We see it as an approach to develop critical awareness and promote socially just language education policies.

References

Braun, V., & Clarke, V. (2006). Using thematic analysis in psychology. *Qualitative Research in Psychology*, *3*(2), 77–101.
Brock-Utne, B. (2010). English as the language of instruction or destruction—how do teachers and students in Tanzania cope? In *Language of instruction in Tanzania and South Africa-highlights from a project* (pp. 77–98). Brill.
Crystal, D. (2002). *Language death*. Cambridge University Press.
Davis, K. A., & Phyak, P. (2016). *Engaged language policy and practices*. Routledge.
Fine, M. (2002). The mourning after. *Qualitative Inquiry*, *8*(2), 137–145.
Freire, P. (1970). *Pedagogy of the oppressed*. Continuum.
Ghimire, N. B. (2019). English as a medium of instruction: Students' discernment in Nepal. *Education and Development*, *29*, 146–160. http://doi.org/10.3126/ed.v29i0.32580
Ghorashi, H., & Wels, H. (2009). Beyond complicity: A plea for engaged ethnography. *Organisational Ethnography. Studying the Complexities of Everyday Life*, 231–251.
Gutiérrez Estrada, M. R., & Schecter, S. R. (2018). English as a "killer language"? Multilingual education in an indigenous primary classroom in Northwestern Mexico. *Journal of Educational Issues*, *4*(1), 122–147.
Hymes, D. (1980). *Language in education: Ethnolinguistic essays*. Center for Applied Linguistics.
Hymes, D. H. (1996). *Ethnography, linguistics, narrative inequality: Toward an understanding of voice*. London: Taylor & Francis.
Khaled, D. Y. A. (2020). English as a killer language: South Africa as a case study. *International Journal of Linguistics, Literature and Translation*, *3*(3), 72–79.
Mathers, A., & Novelli, M. (2007). Researching resistance to neoliberal globalization: Engaged ethnography as solidarity and praxis. *Globalizations*, *4*(2), 229–249.
Ojha, L. P. (2018). Shifting the medium of instruction to English in community schools: Policies, practices and challenges in Nepal. *English Language Teaching in Nepal: Research, Reflection and Practice*. Kathmandu: British Council.
Perez, A. L., & Alieto, E. (2018). Change of "Tongue" from English to a local language: A correlation of mother tongue proficiency and mathematics achievement. *Online Submission*, *14*, 132–150.

Phyak, P. B. (2016). Local-global tension in the ideological construction of English language education policy in Nepal. In R. Kirkpatrick (Ed.), *English language education policy in Asia* (pp. 199–217). Springer International Publishing.

Phyak, P. B. (2021). *Engaged research in applied linguistics: Reflections from practice*. www.aaal-gsc.org/post/engaged-research-in-applied-linguistics-reflections-from-practice

Phyak, P. B., & Bui, T. T. N. (2014). Youth engaging language policy and planning: Ideologies and transformations from within. *Language Policy, 13*(2), 101–119. http://doi.org/10.1007/s10993-013-9303-x

Phyak, P. B., & Ojha, L. P. (2019). Language education policy and inequalities of multilingualism in Nepal. In A. K. A. A. J. Liddicoat (Ed.), *The Routledge international handbook of language education policy in Asia* (pp. 341–354). Routledge.

Phyak, P. & Sharma, B.K. (2020). Functional variations in English: Theoretical considerations and practical challenges. In R. A. Giri, A. Sharma & J. D'Angelo (eds.), *Functionality of English in language education policies and practices in Nepal* (pp. 321–335). Cham: Springer.

Phyak, P., & Sah, P. K. (2022). Epistemic injustice and neoliberal imaginations in English as a medium of instruction (EMI) policy. *Applied Linguistics Review*. http://doi.org/10.1515/applirev-2022-0070

Renshaw, P. D. (2004). Dialogic learning teaching and instruction: Theoretical roots and analytical frameworks. In J. van der Linden & P. Renshaw (Eds.), *Dialogic learning: Shifting perspectives to learning, instruction, and teaching* (pp. 1–15). Springer.

Sah, P. K., & Li, G. (2018). English medium instruction (EMI) as linguistic capital in Nepal: Promises and realities. *International Multilingual Research Journal, 12*(2), 109–123. http://doi.org/10.1080/19313152.2017.1401448

Saud, M. S. (2020a). English medium public schools in Nepal: A new linguistic market in education. *LLT Journal: A Journal on Language and Language Teaching, 23*(2), 319–333.

Saud, M. S. (2020b). Teaching English as an international language (EIL) in Nepal. *Indonesian TESOL Journal, 2*(1), 29–41.

Saud, M. S. (2022, October 15). *Is English in education a medium of instruction or destruction?* [blog post]. http://eltchoutari.com/2022/10/is-english-in-education-a-medium-of-instruction-or-destruction/

Simasiku, L., Kasanda, C., & Smit, T. (2015). Can code switching enhance learners' academic achievement? *English Language Teaching, 8*(2), 70–77.

Skutnabb-Kangas, T. (2010). Language rights. *Handbook of pragmatic highlights. Society and Language Use, 7,* 212–232.

Suliman, A. (2014). The interference of mother tongue/native language in one's English language speech production. *International Journal of English and Education, 3*(3), 356–366.

Thebe Limbu, S. (2021). The making of the English-speaking Nepali citizens: Intersectionality of class, caste, ethnicity and gender in private schools. *Studies in Nepali History and Society, 26*(1):65–96.

Thomas, J. (1993). *Doing critical ethnography*. Sage.

Yin, R. K. (2003). *Case study research: Design and methods* (3rd ed.). Sage.

Index

A1 (code) 52
abductive reasoning, usage 27
Academic Disciplines (AD) 49, 51
acknowledgement, student marking 65
AD1 (code) 52
Agents (A) 51
analytical tools, development 27
animated explanations, multimodal resources (usage) 68
AntConc, usage 51
anti-hegemonic science 116
anxiety, language teacher experiences 7
Arslan, Sezen 94
audio-video recording 79, 80
automated analysis 27
axial coding, usage 97

Babu, Nani 121–123
background noises (technical issue) 81
Barthes, Roland 28
baton (beat) gesture 84
belonging, sense 120
biases, avoidance 79
big data, computational models 27
bilingual programmes 6
blackboard, usage 67
body language, usage (potential) 77
bottom-up conceptual framework, support 46–47

case study, usage 118–120
Chinese-medium instruction (CMI) 33
Ching Cheung, Kason Ka 33
classroom data collection, limitation 80
classroom discourse analysis: epistemic network analysis, usage 33; Excel file, codes (input) *38*; lesson transcript, coding categories **37**; multimodal approaches 19–20; network generation, example *39*
classroom discourse analysis, SFMDA approach 20–26; analysis 24–26; challenges/opportunities 26–28; research planning/design 22–24; theoretical frameworks 20–22; transcription conventions 90
classroom interactions, analysis 35–36; ENA, strengths 39–41; ENA weaknesses, overcoming 41
classroom interactions, usage 3–4
classroom materials, collection 79, 82
classroom observation 79, 80
classroom practices (visualization), multimodal/multichannel analytical framework (usage) 76
classroom research 23–24; data collection 23
classroom resources, collection 79
classroom talk: asymmetrical interactional dynamics 64; proportion, variations 68; student-student interaction, investigation 65
Cloudtagger, usage 89
code-mixing practices 68
codes, distribution **55**
code-switching 68, 72; behaviours 1
Common European Framework of Reference for Languages (CEFR) 83
communicative gestures, ideational meaning 21
concourse, generation 8–9
connected codes, epistemic networks *39*
consensus estimates, usage 55
constructivism, positivism (contrast) 78

Index 129

content: analysis, epistemic network analysis technique 3–4; delivery 100
Content and Language Integrated Learning (CLIL) 33; CLIL-based science classrooms 33–34, 41; English CLIL classrooms, student explanations (analysis) 67; school contexts 66; support, classroom interaction (usage) 3–4
contextual metadata, computational models 27
conversation analysis (CA): affordances 62; approach, importance 4; approach, strengths/focus 63–69; data collection steps **70, 71**; language, interest 19; methodology 63; preparation, steps **70**; stages/steps 69–70; study 68–69
conversation analytic frameworks, impact 66
corpus linguistics: affordances 45, 48–49; combination 51–53; operationalising 48–49; reflexivity/value, demonstration 45–46; usage 45; value 48
critical ethnography, engaged research 120–123
Curle, Samantha 1
Curriculum Genre Theory 23
Curry, Niall 45

data analysis 82–83, 97; example 91–93; unmotivated look 69–70
data collection 96; methods 79
data preparation/analysis/preparation 3
Details, method **3**
Development of disciplinary literacies in English as a lingua franca at university 77–78
Dharmachakra Secondary School (DSS) 120–121
dialogical engagement 116, 123
dialogic approach, usage 123–124
dialogic engagement 118–119, 125
dialogues, questions (discussion) 124
dialogue, usage 124
Diert, Irati 76
disciplinary vocabulary, impact 66
doing knowing (cognitive notions) 66–67
doing understanding (cognitive notions) 66–67
dynamic spatial positions (DSPs) 82

educational multilingual reforms, teacher perceptions 7
education, multimodal turn 19
eigenvalues, significance 11
embodied semiotic resources, study 21–22
EMEMUS. *see* English-medium education in a multilingual university setting
emic (insider) perspective, offering 63
engaged methodological approach 115
engaged research 120–123
engagement: ethnographic monitoring 123–125; situated engagement, case study (usage) 118–120; understanding 115–116
English as a foreign language (EFL), predominance 95
English as Medium of Instruction (EMI) 1, 45; challenges 12; classes, quality (improvement) 101, 103; classroom, experience 20; classroom materials, collection 82; EMI-related keywords/key terms, identification 54; EMI-related policymaking 6–7; lecturer, role 83; practice 6–7; problems 6–7; process, inauguration 6; qualitative research approach, popularity 1; ROAD-MAPPING theoretical framework 4; subjectivity (presence), Q methodology (usage) 6; teaching competence 94–95
English as Medium of Instruction (EMI) classroom talk: CA approach, strengths/potential (focus) 63–69; conversation analysis (CA), affordances 62; conversation analysis (CA) approach, strengths/focus 63–69; conversation analysis (CA), data collection steps **70, 71**; conversation analysis (CA), preparation (steps) **70**; conversation analysis (CA), stages/steps 69–70; explanations, elements (sequence) 67–68; explanations, execution 66–68; interactional dynamics 72; investigation, conversation analysis (affordances) 62;

multimodal resources 72; multiple languages, roles/uses 68–69; multi-unit questions, focus 65; small-group student interaction 72; student-student interaction 64–66; teacher-student interaction 64–66; unplanned word explanations, pattern (identification) 67

English as Medium of Instruction (EMI) instructors: data analysis 97; data collection 96; English use, EMI instructor needs **98**; findings 97–107; fluency 99–100; instructional needs 100–103; instructional-related needs, narrative frames 113; interaction, enhancement 102–103; language needs 97–100, 107–108; language-related components 104–106; language-related needs, narrative frames 113; linguistic/pedagogical needs, narrative enquiry 94; materials/methods 101–102; methods, detail 96–107; narrative frames 100–103, 113; narrative frames, coding (sample) **97**; participants 95–96; participants, demographic distribution **96**; pedagogy-related components 106–107; pedagogy-related needs 107–108; practical lessons 107–109; professional development program components 104–107, 108–109; professional development program components, narrative frames analysis results **104**; project overview/context 94–95; pronunciation 100; research design 96; research planning 95–96; semi-structured interviews protocol 114; study, context 95; suitable words, finding (inability) 98–99

English as Medium of Instruction (EMI) policies: critical ethnography, engaged research 120–123; dialogues, questions (discussion) 124; engagement, ethnographic monitoring 123–125; engagement, understanding 115–116; ideological context 116–118; language ideological meanings, analysis 115; language ideologies study, engaged methodological approach 115; linguistic ideologies, investigation 4; situated engagement, case study (usage) 118–120

English as Medium of Instruction (EMI) research 11–12; audio-video recording 80; classroom materials, collection 82; classroom observation 80; data analysis 82–83; data collection 79–82; design 78–79; details, method 79–83; interviews/focus groups, analysis 46–48; language, extension 76; methodology, example 83–85; planning 77–78; post-semi-structured interviews 81; pre-semi-structured interviews 81; project overview/context 76–77

English as Medium of Instruction (EMI) science classrooms (classroom discourse analysis): epistemic network analysis (ENA), strengths 39–41; epistemic network analysis (ENA), usage 33, 35–39; Excel file, codes (input) *38*; lesson transcript, coding categories **37**; network generation, example *39*; project overview/content 33–34; research context 35; research planning/design 34

English as Medium of Instruction (EMI) stakeholders: case study 53–58; corpus linguistics, affordances 48–49; corpus linguistics methodology, proposal 49–53; data analysis, example 91–93; data/method 53–55; grounded theory 50–51; grounded theory methodologies 48–49; grounded theory methodologies, proposal 49–53; interview/focus group details **54**; interview/focus groups (exploration), corpus linguistics/grounded theory

(usage) 45; keyword analysis 50–51; keywords/key terms **54**; literature review 46–49; methodology, proposal 49–53; research, interviews/focus groups (analysis) 46–48; results/discussion 55–58; ROAD-MAPPING framework 49–50; RO focused codes **57**
English for Specific Purposes (ESP) 2, 76, 89
English Language classroom, lesson microgenres 25
English language competency, development 56
English Language Teachers (ELT) 2
English-medium education in a multilingual university setting (EMEMUS): language, role 61; lectures 46
English-medium instruction (EMI) 33, 76; discursive constructions 47; qualitative research methods 1
English proficiency: problem 108; student improvement 6
English-speaking skills, development 104, 105
English, usage (student unwillingness) 107
English (language), usage 117
English use, EMI instructor needs **98**
Epistemic Network Analysis (ENA) 34; strengths 39–41; technique 3–4; usage 33; weaknesses, overcoming 41
epistemic networks *39*
equity inclusion 72
ethnographically grounded dialogue, usage 123–124
ethnographic data, usage 121
ethnography: philosophy, anti-hegemonic science 116; usage 79
EUDICO Linguistic Annotator (ELAN), development 25
Excel file: codes, input *38*; number, entry 36
explanations: elements, sequence 67–68; execution 66–68
explicit language policy, construction 72

face-to-face (F2F) interviews 81
factor analysis 7–8, 10–11
factor array, presentation 11
factor interpretation 10–11
factor loadings, examination 11
factor matrix, production 12–13
factor rotation 11
feedback, elicitation 27–28
field-specific English education 105; English language support 109
flagging 11
focused codes, application 55
focused coding 97
focus groups 61; top-down/bottom-up analysis 47–48

Gest.R code 41
gestures, types 36
Ghimire, Nani Babu 115
globalisation, trend 1
goal-oriented views 63
Google, usage 89
grounded theory 45, 50–51; adoption 97; combination 51–53; methodologies 48–49; usage 45, 51
group work, epistemic networks *39*

hierarchical power, interpersonal meaning, assertion 24–25
hierarchies, role 50
Higher Education (HE): EMI, usage 12; internationalisation 12, 77–78
hypothetico-deductive approach 8

ICT tools, usage 89
ideational meaning, expression 24
I/F, interrelated actions 64
implicit language policy, construction 72
indeterminacy, embracing 10–11
ING1 (code) 52
Initiation, Response, Evaluation (IRE) 18; IRE/F 64
Initiation, Response, Feedback (IRF) 18
institutional settings, goal-oriented talk 63
instructional needs 100–103
instructors, linguistic/pedagogical needs 94
integrative analytical framework 77
interaction: enhancement 102–103; sequential organisation 63; verbal/multimodal details 62
interactional power, democratic approach 64–65
Internationalisation and Glocalisation (ING) 49–51

internet connection (technical issue) 81
interpersonal meaning 20; expression 24
interpretational sense-making process 27
inter-rater reliability 97
inter-raters, usage 27
interview: analysis, corpus linguistics approaches 45; data, referencing 96; participants, questions 61; top-down/bottom-up analysis 47–48

Jablonkai, Reka R. 62

Ken-Q analysis 10–11; usage 12–13
keyword analysis 50–51
knowledge co-construction 72

L1 academic language, usage 41
L1 academic oral language 36
L1 academic written language 36
L1.Acad.Vocab, usage 40
L1 non-academic language, usage 41
L1 Non-Acad Lang 39
L1.Non. Acad. Lang 39
L1.Non.Acad.Lang code 41
L2 academic language 39; construction (support), representational gesturing (impact) 41
L2 academic oral language 36
L2 academic written language 36
L2 Acad Lang 39
L2.Acad.Vocab 39–40; code 41
L2 everyday oral language 36
L2 non-academic language 39
language: choice, implicit norms (revealing) 68–69; ideologies study, engaged methodological approach 115; learning (support), multimodal representations (example) **42**; needs 107–108; resources 40
Language Management (M) 49, 51
language-related components 104–106
language-related episodes, interaction patterns 72
learning: experience, facilitation 77; sociocultural theories 62–63
lecture, teachers/students (epistemic networks) *39*
Lei, Jun 6
lesson microgenres 25
Lesson transcript, coding categories **37**

LIDISELF project 77–78
Lim, Fei Victor 18
linguistic affordances 77
linguistic cultural diversity 116–117
linguistic inequalities, promotion 118
linguistic nationalism, historical domination 116–117
linguistic needs 94
Linguistics-Plus approach 19

M1 (code) 52
macro analysis 24–25
macro analytical transcription 24
macro themes 51
Mahabharat Secondary School (MSS) 120–121
Mathematical, Physical and Life Sciences (MPLS) 95–96
MAXQDA, usage 25
meaning-making experience 4
meaning-making process, complementing 82
meanings: interpretation 27; tri-metafunctional organisation 26
medium of instruction (MOI) 33
Membership Categorisation Analysis 76
metafunctional meanings, theorisation 22
micro analysis 25
micro-analytic CA approach, affordances (harnessing) 64
microgenres 23
micro-multimodal-multichannel analysis 82
modes, orchestration 77
Moncada-Comas, Balbina 3
monolingual programmes 6
multichannel analysis 82; table template 90
multichannel analytical framework, usage 76
multichannel questions 89
multilingual classroom talk, micro-analytic/moment-by-moment analysis 68
multilingual/multicultural learning contexts 63
multimedia (qualitative analysis), MAXQDA (usage) 25
multimodal analysis, table template 90
Multimodal Analysis Video (MMAV), development 25
multimodal analytical framework, usage 76

multimodal classroom discourse analysis 18–20; conducting 18; study 27–28
multimodal competence 77
multimodal data: nature 26–27; transcription, importance 24
multimodal discourse analysis: approach, application 21; contextualising 23; interpretational sense-making process 27; interpretative exercise 25–26; labour 27
multimodal ensemble, meanings (interplay) 22
multimodality, holistic approach 19
multimodally classroom data, exploration 77
multimodal meanings, interplay 26
multimodal/multichannel ensembles, orchestration (impact) 84
multimodal/multichannel questions 81
multimodal perspective 77
multimodal questions 89
multimodal representations, example **42**
multimodal resources 72; usage 68, 69
multimodal semantics level 19
multimodal transcript 24
multimodal turn 19; experience 76
multiple languages: interaction 72; roles/uses 68–69
multi-unit questions, focus 65
multiword key items, usage 51

narrative frames 95, 100–103, 113; analysis, results **104**; basis 96; coding, sample **97**; interpretation 97; qualitative analysis 107–108; qualitative content analysis, usage 98; usage 97–98
Narrative Positioning 76
natural language processing, computational models 27
Nepal, EMI policy (ideological context) 116–118
Nepali medium of instruction (NMI) 118
Netherlands, secondary school maths classes (explanations analysis) 66–67
networked graphs, usage 25
network generation, example *39*
non-observational methods 79

non-positivist philosophies/epistemologies 8
non-probability sampling strategy 96
non-verbal data, gathering 84
non-verbal materials, usage (potential) 77

off-topic episodes 72; analysis 65
online interviews 81
open coding, usage 97
open-ended responses, production 108
open-source software 25

Pan, Jiahao 6
paralinguistic affordances 77
participant-led subjective expressions/viewpoints 8
PCQ program 10
pedagogical interactions, analysis 18
pedagogical needs 94; achievement 13
pedagogical training 94
pedagogy-related components 104, 106–107, 109
pedagogy-related needs 107–108
Pérez-Paredes, Pascual 45
person-centred approach 7–8, 10
Phyak, Prem 115
pointing gestures (deictic) 36
positivism, constructivism (contrast) 78
post-interview, multimodal/multichannel questions 89
post-semi-structured interviews 81
post-sorting activities 8–10
post-sorting interview/survey 10, 11
PowerPoint presentation 81, 84
PP1 (code) 52
PP, reflections 55
PQMethod 10–11
Practical lessons **3**
Practices and Processes (PP) 49, 51
pre-interviews 81
pre-semi-structured interviews 81
pre-sequence 65
principal component analysis 10–11; usage 12–13
private schools, EMI policy 117–118
professional development programs: adaptation 106; components 104–109; narrative frames analysis results **104**
Project overview/context **3**
P set, interview 12
Pun, Jack K.H. 1, 33

134 Index

Q-concourse, ad hoc framework 9
Q factor analysis 10–11
Q grid 9; 7-point scale, usage 12
qmethod 10–11
Q methodology 2–3, 7–8; quantitative methodology, difference 8; usage 6
Q research 2–3; Stage 1 8–9; Stage 2 9–10; Stage 3 10–11; stages 8–11
Q set 8–9; construction 8
Q-set, statements 13
Q-sort grid, example *10*
Q sorting 108–10
Q sorts: analysis 10–11; analysis, Ken-Q Analysis (usage) 12–13; division 11
Q-sortware 10
Q statements, division 10
Q study, example 12–13
qualitative content analysis, usage 98
qualitative data, obtaining 97
qualitative research: approach, popularity 1; methodology 1–2; methods 4–5
quality education, symbol 117
Quality Management in Tourism (EMI course) 79

ready-made narratives 95
real-life information, providing 80
receptivity, signifying 21
reflective space 115
representational gestures 36
representational gesturing, impact 41
representativeness, importance 48–49
researcher-led objective measurements 8
Research planning/design **3**
RO1 (code) 52, 56
ROAD-MAPPING: application 54; codes 52; codes, distribution **55**; combination 51–53; dimensions 52; focused codes, application 55; framework 45, 49–50; theoretical framework 4
Roles of English (RO) 49, 51; category 57–58; code, unpacking 55; dimension 53; focused codes **57**
Roles of English, Academic Disciplines, Language management, Role of the Agents, Practices and Processes and Internationalisation and Glocalisation (ING) (ROAD-MAPPING) 49, 51–53; application 54

sampling, importance 48–49
scaffolding 72
Science, Technology, Engineering and Mathematics (STEM) courses, comparison 78
scientific proof 25–26
secondary school maths classes, explanations analysis 66–67
selective coding 97
self-repair/non-verbal resources, combination 67
self-reported data/classroom data, integration 77
semiotic choices 28; granular examination 23
semiotic resources, combination 26
semi-structured interviews 81, 95; basis 96; protocol 114; qualitative analysis 107–108; usage 97–98
semi-structured post-interviews 79
semi-structured pre-interviews 79
set epistemological/ontological positioning, absence 50–51
Shrikantha Secondary School (SSS) 120–121
sign-makers, intentions 27–28
Singh Saud, Mohan 115
situated engagement, case study (usage) 118–120
Sketch Engine, usage 51
small-group discussions, student-student interaction (investigation) 65–66
small-group student interaction 72
social inclusion 72
social instructivism, conceptualisation 26
socialisation 120
Social Sciences (SSCC) (Soc) 95–96; courses, comparison 78
spaces, meanings (examination) 22
spatial pedagogy framework 22
speech, linguistic/paralinguistic affordances 77
stanza, defining 36
Stephenson, William 7
structured informality 26
students: English proficiency, impact 94; epistemic networks *39*; language behaviours,

monitoring 117; learning, impact 122; learning process, assistance 84–85; linguistic repertoires 69; positionality, recording 80; teachers, differentiation 36
student-student interaction 64–66, 79; investigation 65
subject disciplinarity 23
subjectivity, understanding 7
subject lecturers, EMI challenges 12
subject-specific terms/knowledge 64
sub-themes: addressing 98; derivation 99
Systemic Functional Multimodal Discourse Analysis (SFMDA) 3, 20; analysis 24–26; approach 20–26; challenges/opportunities 26–28; criticism 35; fine-grained analysis 26–27; research planning/design 22–24; theoretical frameworks 20–22; transcription conventions 90

T2 questions, usage 119–120
talk, micro-analytic/inductive stance 62
teachers: competencies, perceptions 7; epistemic networks *39*; experiences, first-person accounts 95; language behaviours, monitoring 117; talks 1
teacher-student interaction 64–66, 78
Teaching English as a Second Official Language (TESOL) 2
technological tools, usage 84
textual meaning, expression 24
thematic analysis 4; approach 45

thematic coding approaches, usage 45
theory-neutral analysis, absence 26
top-down conceptual framework, support 46–47
transcription: conventions 90; interpretative activity 69; practices, absence 26; processes 51–52
translanguaging 68, 72
tripartite language policy framework 47
trustworthiness, guarantee 79
turn-initial 67
turn-taking, attention 62

unmotivated look 69–70
unplanned word explanations, pattern (identification) 67

variable-centred approach 7–8
Varimax rotation 11; usage 12–13
verbal data, gathering 84
verbal resources, usage 69
VERBI Software 25
video processing, computational models 27
video recording technologies: mass accessibility/affordability 18; usage 23–24
video turn 76
visualisation tools, development 27
vocabulary, usage 105
volume target reader, description 4–5

wh-interrogative question 65
writing, linguistic/paralinguistic affordances 77

YouTube videos, usage 89

For Product Safety Concerns and Information please contact our EU representative GPSR@taylorandfrancis.com
Taylor & Francis Verlag GmbH, Kaufingerstraße 24, 80331 München, Germany

www.ingramcontent.com/pod-product-compliance
Lightning Source LLC
Chambersburg PA
CBHW070552170426
43201CB00012B/1813